PRESENTATION COPY

TO

MARK THE DISSOLUTION

OF THE

COUNTY BOROUGH OF GATESHEAD

ON

MARCH 31st 1974

To...... *Karen Hewitson* ....

A Pupil

at

...... *Hill Head Junior High* ....School

W P Davey

A Short History of Gateshead

I. C. CARLTON, A.L.A.

Adapted from

A History of Gateshead
by
F. W. D. MANDERS, B.A., A.L.A

GATESHEAD CORPORATION
1974

© Gateshead Corporation

ISBN 0 901273 04 X

Printed in Great Britain by
Northumberland Press Limited
Gateshead

CONTENTS

FOREWORD

As Mayor of the County Borough of Gateshead, indeed as the last Mayor of the County Borough, it gives me the greatest of pleasure to write the foreword to this publication.

It affords me an opportunity to address a few words to all the pupils in all the schools in the Town.

In December 1973, the Council published a book, comprising 368 pages and 56 black and white illustrations, entitled *A History of Gateshead* by Mr F. W. D. Manders, B.A., A.L.A., of the Gateshead Public Libraries Department. This book is without a doubt an excellent example of patient and scholarly research, and can be commended both to student and general reader alike.

The Council has decided to present an abridged edition of this book to all children attending schools within the Borough, and this is the volume now in your possession.

In this book you will find the fullest information regarding the County Borough of Gateshead —its origin and growth—its industry and com-

merce—its cultural and leisure activities—its
institutions—its Council—indeed, it is a complete
history of Gateshead.

I hope you will enjoy reading it as much as I
have done.

Leslie Corr

Mayor 1973/74

31st March 1974

PREFACE

As the seventh and last Town Clerk of the County Borough of Gateshead I have been invited to write this preface and I am delighted to accept the honour and privilege

On 1st April 1974, the County Borough of Gateshead will cease to exist. This has come about because of the Re-organisation of Local Government. This re-organisation applies not only to your own Town, but to the whole of England, Scotland and Wales.

So far as this particular area is concerned a new County has been formed, known as the Metropolitan County of Tyne and Wear. This will be governed by a Metropolitan County Council and five Metropolitan District Councils, to be known as Newcastle, Gateshead, Sunderland, North Tyneside and South Tyneside.

Your particular District, to be known as Gateshead, is comprised of the County Borough of Gateshead, the Urban Districts of Felling, Whickham, Blaydon and Ryton, and the Parishes of Birtley and Lamesley. Your present town of Gateshead has a population of approximately 94,000 inhabitants.

The new District of Gateshead will have a population of approximately 235,000 inhabitants. The new Authority will, on 1st April 1974, become a Borough, and will have a Mayor, Civic Regalia, a Mace and a Coat of Arms, just as your old Town has now. Of course the Coat of Arms will be new and different, so as to represent the whole of the new Authority.

As His Worship the Mayor has informed you, *A History of Gateshead* has been published, and you are now presented with this abridged edition.

In this most interesting and comprehensive book, you will find everything you need to know about your present Town—the County Borough of Gateshead.

I hope you will treasure this book, as I do mine.

Robert D Hurst

Town Clerk

31st March 1974

CHAPTER ONE

GATESHEAD THROUGH THE AGES

Unlike some cities and towns, there is very little information available about the ancient history of Gateshead. The town was a minor settlement of little importance, being overshadowed by its larger neighbour, Newcastle. Roman coins were found in Church Street (in 1790) and Bottle Bank (in 1802) so there may very well have been a small camp at the southern end of the old Roman Tyne Bridge. There was, of course, a major Roman fort at Newcastle, and, as was the case in most Roman forts and towns, a small settlement probably grew around the gates at what is now the end of the Swing Bridge, Pipewellgate and Oakwellgate. Little is known of Roman activity in the area around Gateshead, but the exploration of a fort discovered by aerial photographs on Washingwell farm at Whickham may give some clues as to the settlement of the area.

The Venerable Bede, in his *History of the English Church and People*, mentions 'Adda was

brother of Utta, a well-known priest and Abbot
of Gateshead'. The site of the monastery is not
known although old prints of the ruins of what
is now Holy Trinity Church are captioned 'Gate-
side Monastery'. The older part of this building,
formerly St Edmund's Hospital Chapel, was built
about A.D. 1250 but Gateshead was still a very
small settlement. During the Middle Ages Gateshead is described as a place, rather than a vill
(town) or a borough. Real growth began with
the establishment of Norman Bishops of Durham
from 1072. At this time the area now known as
Gateshead was either forest or wasteland with
some agricultural land. The forest, which covered
much of East Gateshead, was used as a hunting
reserve by the bishops of Durham who had a
hunting lodge or manor house in the area, the
theory that the bishops had a palace in Gateshead
is usually discounted. The forest was the subject of
Gateshead's first charter, granted in approximately
1164 by Hugh du Puiset, Bishop of Durham. The
forest was enclosed by a ditch or hedge and rules
were set down for its use by the people of Gateshead. The 'common lands' at Saltwell were also
mentioned; this was probably the same area that
was enclosed in 1814, stretching from the Windmill Hills to the river Team.

Durham was not included in the Domesday
Book, but separate surveys were completed for
the bishopric of Durham which covered most of

Durham and included Gateshead. The first such survey is known as the Boldon Book, made in 1183. Gateshead is listed as having watermills, salmon fisheries on the Tyne and bake-houses. Obviously, the town was not now entirely dependent on agriculture. In the late twelfth century dyeing and shipbuilding are mentioned. At this time, Gateshead was paying a tax of £10 per year to the bishop of Durham, the highest sum for any Durham town.

The appearance of Gateshead was changing, the first man-inspired changes in the town. The forests which had probably covered the area for hundreds of years were being cleared to make way for agriculture. The wastelands of weed and scrub were also being improved. The road from the south did not always follow the old Roman road. The first recorded road ran between the present old and new Durham Roads to enter the town by what is now West Street. A ditch, recorded in 1748, as dividing Low Fell from Sheriff Hill may have been the remains of this road.

Gateshead was growing steadily, if slowly. The first recorded market was held in 1246, while a bailiff is mentioned in a document dated 1287. The bailiff was the representative of the bishop of Durham, the first such officer was Gilbert Gategang. He took advantage of the grants and leases of land of the bishops who were generally losing interest in their Gateshead estates, apart from being a source of revenue, with the result that his family and descendants became comparatively rich. His son, Alan, was known as the Lord of Pipewellgate, which may have been more important than the rest of the town; in 1539 there is a reference to 'Gateshead, near Pipewellgate'.

Throughout the medieval period, the bishops of Durham had to struggle to keep Gateshead as part of their estates. The wealthy merchants and burgesses of Newcastle tried to take control in order to benefit from the increasing trade. The fisheries were often the cause of friction. Those on the south side of the river were destroyed, the catches taken to Newcastle and the fishermen harassed.

The bishop of Durham owned the southern third of the Tyne Bridge: in 1383, this was taken over by the city of Newcastle and a tower was built on it. In 1416, however, the southern portion was returned to the bishop after appeals to the king; usually the bishop won his case at such appeals and investigations but nevertheless, Newcastle was gradually winning the 'war' despite losing these minor skirmishes. 1454 was an important year in this struggle as Newcastle was granted conservatorship of the Tyne, a privilege held for 400 years. This gave that city a monopoly of trade on the river but the coal mines, the main target, were still controlled from Gateshead. The first record of coal being mined in the Gateshead area was in 1344 and there were staiths at Pipewellgate in 1349. The manors of Whickham and Gateshead became the best coal mining areas in Europe and were, of course, the envy of Newcastle merchants.

Eventually there was a takeover. John Dudley, Duke of Northumberland, had had a distinguished military career, but planned to become Lord Protector of new bishoprics of Durham and Newcastle and then, possibly make an attempt on the throne of Edward VI.

Bishop Tunstall of Durham was imprisoned and an Act to annex the manor of Gateshead became law on 30 March 1553. Fortunately, Dudley's plans ended abruptly. Mary became Queen on Edward's death and the conspirator was beheaded. After some opposition, the bishopric was re-established and united with Gateshead on 2 April 1554. In return for his bishopric, Tunstall leased the Saltmeadows on the east of Gateshead to Newcastle for 450 years from 1555. The rent was 44 shillings per year. The amount of land leased gradually increased from 34 acres to 95 acres in 1857 and became an important industrial area from which Gateshead as a town derived little benefit.

Further attempts to take over Gateshead were rebuffed in 1574 and 1576, but by the latter date a small but powerful group of Newcastle merchants had acquired the 'Grand Lease' of the manors of Gateshead and Whickham. The bishop still owned these manors but the terms of the lease were so devised that the ownership was purely nominal, as was the rent. The lease was renewed in 1582 for 99 years. The man who arranged this transaction, one Thomas Sutton (who had considerable influence at the Court in the person of the Earl of Leicester), is reputed to have left for London with two horse loads of money (£12,000) as his reward from the Newcastle merchants.

With the coal mines of Gateshead under the control of Newcastle, the impetus to take over the town was removed and only one other weak attempt was made in 1647. Although Gateshead people had been afraid of control from the north of the river, the town now enjoyed considerable prosperity. The coal mines were exploited as never before and in the hundred years from 1574 coal shipments from Newcastle increased elevenfold while the population of Gateshead doubled to approximately 5,500. However, the lease and the abundant coal supplies ended in 1680. The pits were shallow as problems of ventilation and flooding defeated attempts to mine coal from the deeper seams. Gateshead was now in a state of depression, rents were low and in arrears, the fields were scarred with pit heaps, hindering the cultivation of crops.

The economy of the town was not revived until

the growth of the industrial revolution in the mid-eighteenth century. Steam engines were introduced to clear water from the lower coal seams; glassworks and ironworks created more jobs and Gateshead's fortunes began to improve steadily. The 1830s saw the greatest change in administration of Gateshead. Cuthbert Rippon became M.P., the first for Gateshead, a Town Council was elected in 1835 and the Poor Law Union was set up in 1836. During the same period the Dispensary opened (1832) as did the Mechanics Institute (1836) and a newspaper was published for the first time, the *Gateshead Observer* (1837).

Throughout the nineteenth century the population expanded rapidly; between 1801 and 1901 the increase was 101,291. This expansion was met by a spread southwards of working-class houses. Terrace upon terrace of houses and flats were built over what had been large country estates and the character of the town changed from rural to urban. The descriptions of Gateshead as 'a dirty lane leading to Newcastle' and 'huge dingy dormitory' were partially true during the nineteenth and early twentieth centuries, but the rows of houses which today seem drab were a big improvement on the eighteenth- and early nineteenth-century slums down by the river.

Gateshead was, and is, an industrial town and is easily affected by any recession in trade. An added problem during the nineteenth century was that several thousands worked outside the town but when unemployed, claimed relief from Gateshead's poor rate, even though their previous employers did not contribute to it.

In 1889, Gateshead was made a county borough but in the same year one of the largest employers, Hawks, Crawshay closed down. Unemployment was a burden from this date. Up to the Second World War there were repeated newspaper reports of the unemployed sending deputations to ask the council to provide work. The depression years of the 1920s and 30s created even more unemployment and the Team Valley Trading Estate was built in the mid-1930s to alleviate the situation. The borough boundaries were extended in 1932 to provide more building land and slum clearance was started and is continuing today.

Thousands of council owned dwellings have replaced the earlier substandard housing, new roads within and around the borough will carry the heavy traffic of the future and the former derelict riverside areas have been reclaimed. The appearance of Gateshead has changed, and will change, dramatically.

There are also imminent changes in the administration of the town. In April 1974, Gateshead will merge with Felling, Ryton, Blaydon, Whickham, Lamesley and Birtley to form the Gateshead Metropolitan District Area as part of Local Government Reorganisation. A Royal Commission on Local Government held an enquiry into possible unification of the Tyneside boroughs in 1935. Gateshead was in favour of unification, as the richer authorities (e.g. Gosforth) would help to support the less fortunate areas (e.g. Gateshead). The proposals were very similar to the Metropolitan area of 1974. Other far-seeing ideas of Gateshead at this enquiry were a joint fire service and a Passenger Transport Board for Tyneside, both of which were later put into operation.

CHAPTER TWO

HISTORICAL EVENTS IN GATESHEAD

The history books tend to overlook Gateshead as very little of national significance took place here. However, the history of the town is not without interest, the earliest important event being the murder of Walcher, Bishop of Durham in A.D. 1080. The exact date is known, being recorded as May 14th.

After the Norman Conquest, the North of England proved difficult to control. The border with Scotland had not yet been defined and Saxon nobles used the area as a sanctuary to strike at the invading Normans. The Saxons of the North-East were persecuted as a warning to other unruly persons. There was one exception: Liulph, an ancestor of the Lumley family of Lumley Castle, near Chester-le-Street, was on good terms with Walcher, to the great annoyance of the bishop's Norman advisers. This jealousy resulted in the murder of Liulph. Unlike some bishops, Walcher was a timid cleric, and realising the possible results of this, took refuge in Durham Castle. He sent out messengers proclaiming his innocence and offered to meet and explain to Liulph's relatives. The place chosen was Gateshead, near to St Mary's which stood slightly to the north of the present church.

Walcher came with a large group of followers, obviously a bodyguard, amongst whom were the murderers. A mob gathered, and, urged on by Liulph's family and friends, attacked the Normans. The bishop and his followers took refuge in the church, but those remaining outside were killed. *The Anglo-Saxon Chronicle* gives the figure of one hundred dead. St Mary's was put to the torch and one by one the Normans were forced to leave and were killed. Walcher's pleas were of little avail and with shouts of 'Short rede, good rede, slay ye the bishop' the crowd hacked him to death. (Rede is an Anglo-Saxon word meaning plan or solution, advice or counsel.) His badly mutilated body was eventually recovered by monks from Jarrow and taken to Durham.

This small success encouraged a general uprising, including a brief siege of Durham Castle, but it was short lived and an army under William the Conqueror's half-brother laid waste the area. Gateshead probably suffered badly as it was the scene of the crime.

Mention had already been made of the attempts of Newcastle to annex Gateshead. However, one such attempt deserves to be explained in detail as it shows the collective determination of the town to remain a separate community, apart from the influence of Newcastle.

In 1576, the merchants of Newcastle took the opportunity of the death of the Bishop of Durham, James Pilkington, to press their claim. On 13 March, a bill was introduced to unite the towns and was read in the House of Commons.

The second reading of the bill suffered a delay which allowed the people of Gateshead time to organise resistance to this threat; letters, petitions and statements were issued in their struggles which were eventually successful. The first effort was a petition to Lord Burghley, Lord Treasurer of England, stating their case, explaining the take-over attempts as a means of 'private profit of a few of the said town of Newcastle'. This was followed by a statement of the consequences of such a takeover, mainly comments that Gateshead trade would be acquired by Newcastle to the detriment of the former town. The speaker of the House of Commons, Robert Bell, was the next to be persuaded by Gateshead people. They stated that their town consisted of a great number of 'substantial, honest men, faithful and true subjects, as did appear in the late rebellion', and that if the takeover was allowed to proceed, Gateshead would be 'replenished with evil-disposed persons and thieves'!

As the new bishop had not yet been appointed,

Sir William Fleetwood, Recorder of London, wrote
to Lord Burghley on behalf of Gateshead. Fleetwood was well-known for his law against papists
and in his letter confided to Burghley, 'The town
of Newcastle are all papists, save Anderson'.
Which Anderson is not specified. This letter
signalled the end of the last direct attempt to
annex Gateshead, mainly because the merchants
of Newcastle had acquired the leases of coal mines
on the south bank of the Tyne from 1577, as has
been explained in an earlier chapter.

Gateshead was not situated in a strategic military
position, being at the south of a river while the
danger of attacks from the Scots came from the
north; Newcastle, with its walls and castle guard-
ing a bridge was much more important. Newcastle suffered sieges, but the only record of
Gateshead's involvement was during the Civil
War, when the Scots under General Leslie took
control of the North-East to cut off coal supplies
to London.

It was in August 1644 that the battle of Windmill Hills took place. After Marston Moor, a
Royalist defeat, the Scots had time to try and take
Newcastle, a feat which they had been unable to
accomplish earlier in the year. Approaching from
the south, the Earl of Callender sent a party of
men to clear the way to Newcastle but they met
strong resistance on the Windmill Hills where the
Royalists made a stand. The advance party waited

for the main army to arrive and they easily over-
ran the defenders, chasing them down through
Gateshead and over the bridge to Newcastle.
Cannon were set up on the south bank of the
Tyne to bombard Newcastle, but these in turn
were shot at by the defenders, so Gateshead was
probably damaged by both sides. Five batteries
of cannon were set up on the Windmill Hills, an
ideal site from which to destroy the defences and
the defenders of Newcastle. The occupying forces
destroyed the rectory, left St Mary's in a deplor-
able state, stole cattle and generally disturbed the
way of life of the area. A severe plague added to
these troubles. The battle of Windmill Hills was
really a minor affair when compared with others
in the Civil War, but it was an important event
in the history of Gateshead.

A great disaster to affect Gateshead was the
flood of 1771. Very heavy rain over most of the
North-East caused the Tyne to flow at a higher
level than ever before, six feet above that of 1763.
The scale of the flood can be imagined as the water
level was estimated to be twelve feet above the
spring tide high water mark!

The Tyne rose suddenly during the night of
16/17 November, flooding the lower banks at
each end and demolishing parts of the medieval
Tyne bridge as well as some of the shops which
were built at each side of the bridge roadway.
Some of those who lived on the bridge managed

to escape, others were drowned, but some were dramatically rescued. One family was marooned on a pier with the arches on each side swept away. The hero in this rescue was a Gateshead bricklayer called George Woodward, who noticed that although the arches had been swept away, there were still some shops linking the piers, supported on some timbers. Woodward broke through the walls of each shop until he reached the stranded sufferers and led them to safety.

The rivers Wear and Tees were also in flood, so the North-East suffered badly from this storm. The losses of livestock were heavy, many lives were lost, and communications were disrupted as several bridges were swept away. In fact the only bridge over the Tyne to survive was at Corbridge. Built in 1674, it was reputed to owe its strength to its Roman foundations, but the flat ground to the south allowed some of the flood water to flow around rather than against the bridge. Nevertheless, the townspeople of Corbridge were able to wash their hands in the river while standing on the bridge. At Gateshead, where the banks rise steeply from the river, the bridge had to bear the full weight of a river augmented by the Derwent and Team. One result of the flood was the establishment of a separate post office in Gateshead as easy communication with Newcastle was no longer possible. The first office was at the bridge end and was only meant to provide a temporay ser-

vice, but the new Tyne Bridge took so long to
build that this service was not withdrawn. A
temporary bridge was built, and a ferry service
introduced, but the new bridge was not opened
until 30 April 1781.

There was what was known as 'common land'
near each town and village which was for the
benefit of the inhabitants in that they could graze
their livestock there. These lands were of medieval
origin and in Gateshead covered the area
bounded by Coatsworth Road, Claremont Road,
from there west to Saltwell Road, to Bensham,
west to the river Team, downstream to Low Team
Bridge, up Derwentwater Road to Dixon Street,
then east to Bensham Road taking in Ross Terrace
and Fourth Street, and then up Bensham Road
to its junction with Coatsworth Road. Windmill
Hills and Gateshead Fell were also included. By
the mid-seventeenth century, this 'right of
common' had been taken over completely by the
borough-holders and freemen for their own benefit,
a privilege which they jealously guarded. The
freemen declined in numbers until the borough-
holders were to the fore. In August 1807 they
decided to enclose Gateshead Fell so that each
member would have his own land, rather than
share the whole Fell with others. Obviously, there
were considerable conflicting interests with the
result that the area was not divided until December 1822. Similar events affected Bensham. In May

1813 the borough-holders decided to look into the possibility of dividing the rest of the town fields. The necessary Enclosure Act was passed on 28 June 1814, and the fields were divided in 1818 and so this ancient right came to an end. These fields and plots were quickly sold as building land over the next three decades. The Windmill Hills remained in the possession of the borough-holders until 1861 when they were conveyed to Gateshead Corporation to form the first public park in the town.

The year 1832 was notable as far as coal mining was concerned. The miners had no union and were determined to form such a group to struggle for better conditions of employment. On the other hand, their employers, the colliery owners, were just as determined to break the union and therefore employed men who were not members, known as 'blacklegs'. The miners' houses were the property of the colliery owners and they were needed for the new, non-union, workers. The efforts of the police to eject the striking pitmen from their homes led to several unpleasant incidents, one of which took place at Friars' Goose at East Gateshead. The miners had been urged to keep the peace and behave in an orderly manner but the attitude of the police and bailiffs was enough to cause riots and bloodshed.

A large body of miners had assembled at the colliery to meet the police. The leader of the policemen, a Mr Forsyth, issued two cartridges of swan-shot to each of his men and then proceeded with his unpleasant task. The miners were enraged by the taunts of the police and the damage to their furniture, so, while the 'ejectors' were in the house of a Mr Carr, they overpowered the sentry of the building designated as the police headquarters and stole his guns. In the ensuing chaos the police were trapped in a narrow lane. Unfortunately, the lane was overlooked by a small hill on which some miners stood and threw stones and other missiles. Realising their predicament, they fired on the crowd and the miners fired back inflicting several casualties during the police retreat to the safety of some rising ground. Messengers were sent to bring soldiers from nearby Newcastle, but the pitmen realised the plan and obstructed their passage as much as possible so that when the military arrived, accompanied by the Mayor of Newcastle and the Rector of Gateshead, the rioters had dispersed. Not to be outdone, the forces of the law arrested more than 40 innocent people, including three women, accompanied by considerable police brutality. This episode is known as the 'Battle of Friars' Goose'.

The coal owners of the area bribed the constables with beer so that those stationed in pit villages often used unnecessary and unwarranted violence against the strikers. No doubt Friars' Goose suffered as badly as any.

The greatest disaster to strike Gateshead was the Great Fire. There had been plagues and fires before 1854 but this was by far the greatest conflagration Tyneside had ever seen. It began in the early morning of Friday 6 October, in a worsted factory in Hillgate. The alarm was raised by a policeman in Newcastle at about 12.30 a.m. and such fire fighting equipment as was available was brought into use. Despite this the fire raged virtually unchecked. There was a large, seven-storey warehouse very close to the fire used for storing sulphur, nitrate of soda and other combustible chemicals. The sulphur began to melt and although this warehouse had been designed to withstand fires, this conflagration proved too great and soon the warehouse and nearby buildings were blazing. Soldiers and volunteers from the gathering crowds were now helping the firemen.

There were two small explosions but people were preoccupied with the fire. Then at 3.10 a.m. a terrific explosion blew up the warehouse, sending flaming sulphur and timber over the river to Newcastle. It is recorded that some wood and stones had been blown over half a mile away. The noise was heard from as far away as Hartlepool, Hexham and Alnwick, gas lamps were blown out at Jarrow and the flames could be seen from Northallerton. The High Level and Tyne Bridges shook, no doubt to the great alarm of the crowds which had chosen them as a vantage point from which to view the fire.

The fire had now spread to Newcastle and help was sent for from Berwick, Sunderland and even Carlisle. Horse drawn fire engines were brought from all over the North-East. The fire continued to spread in Gateshead, threatening the badly damaged St Mary's Church. It was only brought under control by army sappers and miners blowing up buildings in its path. Spectators came to look at the damage, special trains ran on the following Sunday bringing 20,000 people into Newcastle and Gateshead. Some time later in the year, Queen Victoria asked that her train be stopped on the High Level so that she and her family could look for themselves. More than fifty people were killed and 200 families were made homeless, many of them from the poorer classes who lived in the slums near the river. There were several stories concerning narrow escapes during the disaster. People were said to have sat up in bed at the sound of the explosion and seconds later a stone came through the roof landing amongst the pillows.

A fireman and his son were standing together at the scene of the disaster. The fireman was killed during the explosion but the son survived. The estimated damage was put at more than £500,000 but only one quarter of this was paid out in insurance cover. As well as the large crater in Gateshead and fire damaged buildings, many windows were blown out.

A Presbyterian Minister from South Shields wrote a sermon which said that this calamity was a divine judgement for the ungodliness of the people! Copies went on sale and profits were given to the relief fund. This raised more than £10,000 thanks to special collections, a charity theatre performance and large donations, including £100 from the Queen. Compensation was paid at a rate of £50 per family, probably making some poor families much better off than they were before the fire.

Official inquests were carried out in Gateshead and Newcastle and rumours that gunpowder had been stored in the warehouse were discounted. Experiments were carried out to find the cause of the explosion and experts were called in, but both juries decided that there was insufficient evidence to point to any particular cause. If any good can be said to have resulted from the fire, it was that the shocking slums of Hillgate were largely destroyed and were never rebuilt. The area destroyed by the fire may be seen to this day.

CHAPTER THREE

HISTORICAL ASSOCIATIONS OF GATESHEAD

When one looks at Gateshead in 1974, there appears to be very little to remind anyone of the town in past centuries. The town centre was not developed by celebrated builders such as Dobson and Grainger, but nevertheless, rural Gateshead was a popular residential area for Newcastle's merchants, away from the slums on *both* sides of the river. However most of our old buildings have been demolished, either for health reasons or general development.

Let us go on a tour of Gateshead as it was in the late eighteenth and early nineteenth centuries before the rapid increase in the size of the town. There was only one bridge over the Tyne, occupying the site of the present Swing Bridge. From this new bridge, opened in 1781, one could see most of the town clustered along the riverbanks and up the steep slope of Bottle Bank to what were then the outskirts of Gateshead; now the town centre.

Pipewellgate and Hillgate were narrow streets,

the former only eight feet wide, even though they had been recently rebuilt, and as in later years, industry was to be found here alongside houses. Gas works, glass works, lime kilns, a glue factory and a tannery were situated in Pipewellgate.

The main road to Durham led up Bottle Bank, named after the Saxon word 'botl' meaning settlement. This was and, of course, still is a very steep hill. Church Street was built in 1790 to alleviate this problem and follows the same course as today, curving to the east, passing St Mary's, and then rejoining Bottle Bank at the foot of High Street. Behind these main streets were alleys and courts with poor drainage and no sanitation. The living conditions were poor, of course, but not as bad as the overcrowding later in the century when cholera, typhoid and smallpox raged. There were some fine houses fronting on to the main streets but as their owners deserted them for more salubrious surroundings to escape from the squalor of these courts, the once fine houses were tenemented and became slums.

Once he had left the river, the traveller in 1800 would soon find himself amongst houses with large gardens and fine country views. On the east of High Street, the houses with courts, alleys and streets behind continued almost as far as Jacksons Chare (Jackson Street), but on the west there were gardens and an orchard on the site of the shopping precinct and multi-storey car park. Barns

Close was fields and Bailey Chare, later Half Moon Lane and now Mulgrave Terrace, was a country road leading from High Street to the Windmill Hills and giving the traveller fine views of the Tyne Valley. There were some houses on West Street and a windmill at its junction with Jackson Chare where the Co-operative Store stands today.

St Edmund's Hospital Chapel, now Holy Trinity Church, stood among trees in a field, a picturesque ruin. Nearby, Park Lane lived up to its name, passing between fields to Park House and its estate. There were further scattered houses along High Street; one small terrace on the west side was called Pleasant Row, probably indicative of a pleasant place in which to live. To the east of the junction of Sunderland Road and High Street were two reservoirs which supplied some of the town with water. There had been ponds on this site, filled by a stream flowing from the west called the Busy Burn. This area is now covered by the A1 flyover and the now derelict All Saints School and playing field. Further south, opposite the Five Bridges Hotel, stood King James' Hospital, which was in fact an old peoples' home, an institution which still exists: new buildings have been opened on Sunderland Road. This part of High Street, known then as Brunswick Street and now Old Durham Road, was the site of St Edmund's Church, while the land between the

Old and new Durham Roads was an extensive market garden.

The rest of Gateshead, apart from Sheriff Hill, was given over to agriculture although industry was beginning to make its mark along the South Shore and coal mines were scattered throughout the area. There were still large, private estates covering most of the town. The largest was the Park Estate which at 424 acres in 1836 was the remnant of the bishops of Durham's hunting park to the east of Gateshead. It had been much larger than this with boundaries of High Street, Split Crow Road, Felling boundary and the Tyne. Shipcote Estate was also large, originating from the former estate of St Edmund's Hospital. The boundaries can be defined as follows: from the Co-operative Store on High Street south to Charles Street, east to High Street, south along High Street and Old Durham Road as far as the Old Cannon Inn, from here to Kells Lane, west down through Beaconsfield Road and Whinney House Dene, north to a point in line with Bewick Road where the boundary ran eastwards to Alexandra Road, north along East Park Road and Avenue Road to Westfield Terrace, west down Westfield Road and Westminster Street to Saltwell Road, north to Bensham Road and then east to High West Street. The Redheugh Estate was one of the oldest in the town, set up as early as the thirteenth century by the Redheugh family. It consisted, apart from

some small areas, of the land between the town
fields at Bensham and the Tyne. In its heyday
Saltwell Estate had been the largest in Gateshead
covering approximately 500 acres, extending from
East Park Road to the Team and from Bensham
to Low Fell. In 1805 this area was split up into
several smaller groups, one of which, the Saltwell Cottage Estate, forms the present Saltwell
Park.

Other small estates filled the gaps between these
larger entities. Rodsley and Field House were
spread over the area between the park, Saltwell
Road, Alexandra Road and Westfield Terrace
west to Saltwell Road. They were divided by what
is now Rectory Road with Field House on the
west. Deckham was another small estate bounded
by Split Crow Road, Old Durham Road, Carr Hill
Road and Hendon Road. These estates passed
from family to family and varied in size throughout the centuries. For example, Field House
Estate to the west of the park only covered 44
acres when it was built over from 1894 but earlier
in the century it had been four times as large.
Part was added to Saltwell Cottage Estate and
another 31 acres became Rodsley Estate. The
boundaries can be traced easily in most cases by
reference to modern streets. This is no coincidence
as most of the land was sold for building, and
naturally, houses were built right up to the boundaries so that the developers, often local trades-

men, could extract the maximum income from their investment.

These estates had mansions built for and occupied by the wealthy manufacturers who had left their own industrial squalor on the banks of the Tyne. In turn, the big houses were abandoned as the spread of terraced houses destroyed the privacy of the formerly secluded grounds. Redheugh Hall was a typical example of this. The Hall was of seventeenth-century origin (standing approximately 200 yards west of the Redheugh Bridge, just above the Tyne) and was bought by George Hawks as a country retreat within easy reach of his factories in Gateshead. However, the Teams and Redheugh areas were built over spoiling the privacy of the area and Hawks moved to another country house at Pigdon near Morpeth. There is a print of Redheugh Hall in the Local History and Archives Collection in the Central Library showing a fine house surrounded by trees and gardens (Reproduced in this book). There is also a photograph taken in 1910 when the same building was desolate and deserted, a sad comparison. It was finally demolished in 1935/6. Other halls, houses and mansions suffered a similar fate; Deckham Hall off Carr Hill Road was demolished in 1930; Bensham Hall and Tower to the east of Saltwell Road in the 1890s; Field House at the southern end of Ferndene Road in 1931; Saltwell Hall in Saltwell Cemetery in 1936; Saltwell

Towers still stands in the park, but the woodwork suffers from dry rot and it is now unused. South Dene Tower stood where the crematorium is situated and was the model for Saltwell Towers. South Dene was damaged when used as an A.R.P. station during the 1939-45 war and was later used as flats for a time before being demolished in 1953.

The street names of Gateshead are reminders of buildings, people, places and events in the history of the town, Coatsworth Road is named after William Cotesworth, lord of the manor in the early eighteenth century. He lived in Park House which was rebuilt in 1719-20 by Cotesworth and later in 1728-30 by the Ellison family. This once fine house still stands (January 1974) but forms part of the Clarke, Chapman—John Thompson Engineering Works. The derivation of Windmill Hills is obvious. It was an ideal site for windmills, being on a hill to catch sufficient wind to turn the sails. There were about ten mills on this site which covered a much larger area than today, stretching over to the 'stony flatt', the flat brow of the hill which is now Coatsworth Road.

There were others mills in the town: the last to be demolished was Snowdon's Mill at Carr Hill in 1964, but their memory has been preserved in names of public houses such as the 'The Five Wand Mill'. Windmill Hills was the town's first public park, given to the people of Gateshead on

18 November 1861, but it had been a park in all
but name for some years before this. As an open
area near to the town centre it was used for fairs
or 'hoppings', sports days, concerts, election meetings as well as being a pleasant place to go for a
walk. Holly House, one of the town's oldest buildings still standing is situated on the north-east of
the hills. Reputed to have been built in the seventeenth century, it was altered in the late eighteenth
century. It was used as a private house until the
beginning of the twentieth century when it was
bought by the Corporation and used as a reception
centre by the Welfare and Social Services Department. It was abandoned in 1971 and now stands
vandalised and derelict but it cannot be demolished without the permission of the Department of
the Environment. A campaign to preserve the
house has attracted the attention of the local press
but at the time of writing there are no plans for
any restoration work.

Ellison Street is named after the Ellison family
who were Lords of the Manor from 1730-1857. The
best known member of the family was Cuthbert
Ellison (1783-1860) M.P. for Newcastle from 1812
to 1830. Although he lived at Hebburn and London
for the latter part of his life, he gave generously to
many Gateshead charities.

Sheriff Hill is so called from the custom whereby
the Sheriffs from Newcastle came to what is now
Sheriff Hill to meet the judges from Durham

coming north to hold assizes. At that time the area
was little more than barren waste and moor with
some miserable hovels and cottages and the Old
Cannon Inn which was used as a place of refresh-
ment during the judges' journey.

Half Moon Lane acquired its name in an unusual fashion. The street was originally a narrow
alley known as Bailey Chare but in the early
nineteenth century it was widened to allow the
passage of wheeled vehicles. A stone mason and
sculptor named Jopling wanted the new street to
be called 'Marble Street' and fixed this name on
the front of his premises which stood where the
approach is to the High Level Bridge. The inn-
keeper of the Half Moon Inn was a Mr Birch, a
retired comedian who had become a publican
after marrying the daughter of the previous landlord. Birch objected to 'Marble Street' and his
choice, 'Half Moon Lane' was put on his premises.
Eventually, Jopling died and a Mr Murray took
over the premises as a chemist's shop, fixing a
signboard over 'Marble Street' and so in due
course Half Moon Lane became accepted as the
only name. In 1847 the old houses were demolished
to make way for the present street.

There are some local legends which have interesting historical associations. There was an old
stone house known as 'King John's Palace' at the
southern end of Oakwellgate. This tradition is
now discounted but J. R. Boyle, the historian, has

put forward the theory that this house may have
been on the site of the old manor house of the
bishops of Durham as it is very close to what was
once their forest and hunting park to the east of
the town. At one time the house was known as
'Palace Green'.

Daniel Defoe is often said to have written his
famous novel *Robinson Crusoe* in Gateshead. He
was a resident for a brief period around 1710,
staying in Hillgate with one Joseph Button, a book-
seller with a shop on the old Tyne Bridge. However, it is now thought that this book was written
in Stoke Newington. The first part was published
some nine years after he left Gateshead.

Another tradition is that Charles I stayed in
Gateshead at a house in Oakwellgate known as
the 'Bush Inn'. Part of the building was later to
form a public house of that name and the rest was
used as the first Town Hall in Gateshead. It is
now demolished and the site is occupied by a
garage behind which is a yard still known as Bush
Yard. It seems highly unlikely that Charles I
would have stayed in Oakwellgate even though it
was one of the better areas of the town. He would
travel with a considerable retinue which would
not have been adequately housed in Gateshead
at that time. One would have thought that the
king would have preferred to stay in the more
secure and spacious houses in Newcastle.

Despite the wholesale redevelopment and slum

clearance which has demolished most of older
Gateshead, there are still historical buildings
worthy of note. The two oldest churches are St
Mary's and Holy Trinity. Each of these churches
is said to have been built on the site of Gateshead
monastery but there is nothing to show its exact
location. The monastery may have been attacked
and destroyed by the Vikings, but this is a matter
of conjecture. Nevertheless, St Mary's is a very old
church. The well-known historian, John Hodgson,
who was once a curate at St Mary's, thought that
as some of the stones were shaped or hewed after
the Roman style, they could have been taken from
an old Roman building. In 1080 the bishop of
Durham was murdered in St Mary's, but this
church is traditionally said to have been situated
slightly to the north of the present building.
St Mary's church has been burnt down, restored
and altered several times during the years since the
Norman Conquest so that very little of the original
structure remains. The present tower was built
in 1738-40, while in 1854, during the great fire of
Gateshead, the church was so badly damaged that
there were proposals to demolish what was left and
build an entirely new church. Fortunately, this
plan was not carried out but the twelfth-century
chancel and stained glass windows were beyond
repair. St Mary's still remains as a clearly visible
link with Gateshead's historic past, the 'Mother
Church' of the town.

The oldest part of Holy Trinity Church in High Street is the south aisle. This was originally the chapel of the Hospital of St Edmund, founded in about 1248, and later became a branch of the Convent of St Bartholomew, believed to be Newcastle's oldest religious establishment. Along with other institutions, St Edmund's suffered during the dissolution of monasteries in 1536-40. It remained in a ruinous condition until 1836 when Cuthbert Ellison gave it to the Rector and Churchwardens of Gateshead. A public subscription raised sufficient money for restoration which was carried out under the supervision of John Dobson and Holy Trinity church was opened in 1837. The church today stands in a busy street, passed by thousands who do not know of its historical connections. It was close to Holy Trinity that a Roman Catholic priest was martyred for his beliefs in 1595. There was formerly a cross on the site.

There is a list of buildings to be preserved for historical or architectual reasons. There are nineteen remaining in Gateshead in several grades. The only grade one (most important) building is the High Level Bridge. We could hardly do without it! Several churches are included as well as the Housing Department at the corner of Nelson Street and West Street, donated by the Swinburne family and used as the Dispensary from 1855. The printing works of Robert Kelly Ltd. at the junction of Ellison Street and West Street is a grade three building. It was opened in 1837 as a Congregational Church, then became a Presbyterian Church in 1845. It has been used as a printing works since 1895. By coincidence, another local printing firm, Howe Brothers, occupied the former Bethesda Methodist New Connexion Chapel in nearby Melbourne Street. It was at this latter chapel that William Booth, later to found the Salvation Army, was given his first permanent post. The Bethesda Chapel was demolished in 1964.

Two public houses are worthy of note. The 'Queen's Head' in High Street (a grade three building) and the 'Half Moon Hotel' (unlisted) are generally recognised as the oldest in the town although both were rebuilt in the nineteenth century, the 'Queen's Head' was rebuilt in 1854 and the 'Half Moon' in 1891. The rebuilding of the latter was necessitated after one of Gateshead's early steam trams ran out of control in High Street and demolished the hotel which had been showing all the signs of old age. The compensation paid to the owner must have been considerable as the 'Half Moon' was rebuilt as a much improved establishment. It was obviously a most fortunate accident!

Oakwellgate Baths, opened in 1855, still stand today (January 1974). These were Gateshead's first public baths and wash-houses and cost £4,300 to build. The washing facilities included 'ingenious' wringing machines and about 400 people per week made use of them, but the baths were expensive and were therefore little patronised. The charges were as follows: warm baths—first class sixpence; second class twopence; cold baths —twopence and one penny respectively while washing was charged for at one penny per hour.

Industrial archaeology is a growing branch of historical study and there are relics of Gateshead's industrial past to be seen. The most famous, of course, is the High Level Bridge. The main contractors were Hawks and Co. of Gateshead. The railway bridge over the road on the Newcastle side of the High Level bears a plaque naming Abbot & Co. of Gateshead as the builders in 1848. The route of the Brandling Junction Railway can be seen from the Redheugh Bridge, climbing the river bank towards Greenesfield and passing under the approaches to the King Edward Bridge. The river banks to the east of Gateshead were, of course, leased to Newcastle and were the main industrial areas of the town. Much of the dereliction has now been cleared and a park and industrial estate have been created on a former chemical waste heap. There were also collieries here and due to the proximity of the river, they needed a steam engine to pump the workings dry. The old engine house of one of these pumps can still be seen in the riverside park at Friars' Goose.

CHAPTER FOUR

HOW GATESHEAD WAS
GOVERNED

After the Conquest of 1066, the Norman kings
found that the North-East was difficult to govern
and defend. The one person in a position to
assist the king was the bishop of Durham, and
from the twelfth century onwards the bishops
became increasingly powerful and gained many
royal privileges. The Palatinate of Durham which
was formed became, in effect, a kingdom within
a kingdom, with the Prince Bishop as its ruler.

Gateshead was one of the palatinate boroughs in
1180; and until the sixteenth century was governed
by a bailiff, as the bishop's representative. The
bailiff, who was usually a member of a local landed
family, supervised several executive officers—a
steward, a sergeant of arrest, and four wainmen
who collected the toll on wagons and carts passing
through the borough. The bailiff was also responsible for forwarding the revenue of the town to the
bishop, and for holding the borough courts.

The borough court was the main institution of
government in the town until the seventeenth

century. It depended for its operation on the burgesses of Gateshead, who were the owners of certain houses and lands in the town which carried with their ownership a 'borough right'. These burgesses, who later became known as borough-holders, attended the borough court, which was normally held every two weeks, where they made bye-laws for the government of the town, under the guidance of the bailiff. A document of 1576 claimed that 'the town of Gateshead is ruled by bailiff and burgesses, and hath good and whole-some constitutions and ordinances within them-selves, and is as well governed for justice as they are in Newcastle, punishing all offenders who cast rubbish and cleansing of their homes into the river of Tyne...'

The above was written during one of the periodic attempts by the town of Newcastle to annex Gateshead and sever it from the bishopric of Durham. The first of these attempts took place in 1553, after three centuries of harassment of Gateshead merchants and traders by their opposite numbers in Newcastle, who desired to control ship-ping on both sides of the Tyne. An added attraction of Gateshead was the rich seams of coal which were being mined there. How Gateshead was annexed has already been described but the complete takeover was short-lived. However, by 1599 Gateshead was firmly controlled by its larger neighbour to the extent that the bailiffs of Gateshead during the first half of the seventeenth century were appointed not by the bishop of Durham, but by the Common Council of New-castle.

This period of control by Newcastle, when the bishop's local authority was very weak, seems to have resulted in the growth of a more local type of administration—the select vestry of St Mary's Parish Church, known as the four-and-twenty. As its name suggests, this select vestry comprised twenty-four of the leading inhabitants of Gates-head, who were self-co-opting, not elected by the parishioners, and who effectively controlled those aspects of local government—for example the care of the poor, the maintenance of the highways— which government legislation had made a parish responsibility. The minute books of the four-and-twenty survive from 1626, when the body was already well-established. The four-and-twenty met at St Mary's Church each Easter and appointed the various parish officers—churchwardens, overseers of the poor, overseers of the highways, and four parish constables. By 1658, the power of the four-and-twenty was so great within the town that it was necessary to obtain an Order in Council from Oliver Cromwell himself to have them removed from office when they disagreed with the Puritan minister at St Mary's, Thomas Weld.

By 1679, with the easily obtainable coal in Gateshead almost worked out, the bishop of

Durham regained direct control of the town. By 1684, however, he had decided to abandon direct control of Gateshead through his bailiff and instead to lease the manor to private individuals in return for an annual rent. From 1730 until 1857 the lordship of the manor of Gateshead was held by various members of the Ellison family.

The borough courts were replaced by manor courts, although this change of name did not result in a change of function. The court could fine townspeople for having their shop fronts out of repair, for selling short-weight goods, for dung-hills in the streets and for encroaching on their neighbour's land. For example, a Mrs Maddison was fined for 'allowing her servants to team filthy water out at the back side of her house', and the improbably named Cornelius Quack for 'building a Jakes House (privy) in the Common Landing'.

Throughout these changes in administration, the borough-holders had retained their power and influence, based on their property. In addition, since the seventeenth century, they had taken over the administration of the Town Fields at Bensham and on Gateshead Fell. In this they were joined by the freemen who were members of the guilds or trade companies which had been set up from the sixteenth century. By the eighteenth century the Town Fields were no longer 'common' to all the people of Gateshead as they had once been; they were run as a commercial proposition by the

relatively small number of borough-holders and
freemen.

By the middle of the eighteenth century the
four-and-twenty was in decline; at the annual
meeting in 1745 only three out of twenty-four
were present. Although they continued to appoint
the parish officers, on more than one occasion a
matter of major importance was decided at a
meeting which was attended by the inhabitants
of the town at large. In 1833 there was an
abortive attempt to challenge the authority of the
four-and-twenty, but the townspeople were so
apathetic (only three people attended a parish
meeting in 1830) that the powers of the four-and-
twenty were gradually eroded, not as a result of
local effort, but by various legislative measures
which removed duties from the parish. As early as
the 1770s it was realised that the various units of
local government, the manor court, the borough-
holders and freemen, and the four-and-twenty,
were either too inefficient or self-interested to provide a good local administration. In 1772 and
again in 1791, groups of Gateshead people
requested the bishop of Durham to re-appoint a
bailiff, but their petitions were ignored.

In 1833, Gateshead's local administration was
investigated by a Parliamentary Commission, and
despite fierce opposition from the borough-holders
and freemen, the town became a municipal
borough under an Act of Parliament of 1835; the

first election of Councillors was held on 26 December 1835, and on 1 January 1836, George
Hawks was elected Gateshead's first Mayor. Early
meetings of the new Borough Council were held
in the Anchorage at St Mary's Church, until a
house in Oakwellgate was rented. In 1844 a building near Greenesfield was bought and used as a
Town Hall until 1867, when it was demolished
to make way for the Team Valley Extension Railway. While the new Town Hall was under construction in West Street, the Council met in premises in Queen's Head Yard. The foundation stone
of the new building was laid by R. S. Newall, the
rope manufacturer, in June 1868 and the Town
Hall was opened amid great ceremony in February
1870. The building, surmounted by a statue of
Queen Victoria, has recently been cleaned of
decades of grime and must look much as it did
when new.

Throughout the nineteenth century, the responsibilities, and consequently the cost, of the Borough
Council slowly increased. In the first year of its
existence total payments made by the council
amounted to only £311. Most of this was spent
on the police, street lighting and the maintenance
of roads. Additional duties were added, such as
public health, parks, public libraries and education. There was always considerable resistance
from ratepayers to the increasing cost of local
government in Gateshead: it was not until after

the First World War that the Council began to build houses for rent, although this had been suggested as an answer to Gateshead's housing problem in the 1890s.

Gateshead had a very low rateable value in relation to its population, which meant that very little could be done to improve the state of the town until assistance was available in the form of Government grants.

Gateshead became a County Borough in 1889 and was granted a Coat of Arms in 1932 which was very similar to those (entirely unofficial) arms which had been used for some years—the goat's head was usually prominent.

Various schemes of local government reform for Tyneside were proposed in 1935, 1962, and 1968, but they were mainly exploratory exercises. Finally, in 1973, the Metropolitan Council of Tyne and Wear was formed, and Gateshead, with its neighbours Felling, Whickham, Blaydon and Ryton, together with the parishes of Birtley and Lamesley forms one of the five districts of the Metropolitan area.

CHAPTER FIVE

SOCIAL CONDITIONS IN GATESHEAD

Some Aspects of Everyday Life in Gateshead
Today, it is hard to imagine a medieval Gateshead,
with markets and fairs, ancient buildings and
narrow thoroughfares but the Vestry minute books
of St Mary's church give an insight into almost
every aspect of life in the town. It would seem
that Gateshead was a fairly typical English community, right down to the provision of stocks for
the correction of the criminal element. The church
and parish were the centre of community life;
people were more religious, attending church
regularly, and the parish was the unit of local
government.

As the unit responsible for law and order, Gateshead parish was fined a sum of 6/8 by the justices
of the peace in 1627 because it did not possess a
ducking stool. This omission was rectified in 1628
at a cost of 12/-. This ducking stool, traditionally
used for the punishment of scolding wives, was
soon worn out and was replaced in 1660. Whipping
was another device used in the defence of the

law as well as a means of discouraging poor
people and vagrants from staying within the town
and so placing an extra burden on the parish funds.
However, this deterrent did not prove absolute,
as the burial registers often list 'a poor unknown
stranger' who was interred in a parish coffin at a
cost of 1/4d. Some economies were effected as
these coffins were used over and over again!
Witches and sorcery have been the cause of considerable superstition during the centuries. Witch
hunts were common and the only punishment
was death. Gateshead had witches: in 1649-50
several were arrested, imprisoned, tried at
Durham, executed and buried, all for £2–0–10d.
Yes, these were the 'good old days'. However, life
had its happier moments. The annual riding of
the boundaries was an important social event,
especially for the small boys who fought over figs
and prunes thrown down by the passing cavalcade.
When the town fields were mown, or the streets
relaid, fiddlers or pipers were provided to enter-
tain the workers—the provision of music to improve working conditions is not a recent innovation. There were 'sports' as well, bull-baiting,
cock-fighting and archery were the order of the
day instead of football. The site of the present bus
station at Wellington Street was known as 'the
Butts', possibly indicating the place where the
mandatory archery practice took place.

Education was virtually non-existent in Gates-

head until the nineteenth century when national
schools, and from 1870 board schools, were provided. The Anchorage school was held in the
parish room attached to St Mary's church, from
which the institution was named. This name in
turn was derived from anchoress, a female hermit,
for whom a cell was built beside the church in
the fifteenth century. The number of pupils was
limited by the size of the building and the wealthi-
est families sometimes preferred to send their
children to private schools elsewhere; for example,
Henry Ellison sent his sons to Eton.

Markets were held from the early thirteenth
century and by 1336 there were two each week,
on Tuesdays and Thursdays, as well as an annual
fair held on the first of August. These activities
appear to have ceased in 1647 when the influence
of Newcastle resulted in a general decline in the
independence of Gateshead. However, towards
the end of that century, an annual shoe fair was
established which attracted traders from all parts
of the North-East. This continued until 1853
when only one stall was set up, although the fair
had been a shadow of its former self for several
years beforehand.

A street scene in old Gateshead was similar to
that of many other English towns: the old houses
would be stepped out over the narrow thoroughfares, which were filled with traders, carriages and
carts, animals being driven to the slaughterhouse

or markets, and rubbish. The streets in those days served as sewers, drains and rubbish dumps. One such heap cost £4.00 to be removed although the contractors paid 10/- for the rubbish itself. The size of this, which had accumulated over four years, can be gauged by the cash involved, and although exact dimensions cannot be given, it must have been very large! People did not realise that such uncleanliness bred germs and the town was frequently visited by the plague.

From the lords of the manor in their mansions to the miserable beggars in the streets, the people of Gateshead and their activities represent a cross section of life in England over the centuries.

Social Services
During the middle ages, the poor were cared for by charities, both private and ecclesiastical until legislation in 1559 and 1601 made relief of the poor one of the responsibilities of the parish authorities but church hospitals existed after this time: In Gateshead there were the hospitals of St Edmund, Bishop and Confessor, and St Edmund, King and Martyr. The dates of their foundation are unknown but they are known to have existed in 1247 and 1315 respectively. The history of St Edmund, Bishop and Confessor, is the more obscure of the two. It was connected with the convent of St Bartholomew of Newcastle and suffered badly during the campaigns of Henry

VIII against the Catholic Church. Only the chapel
of the hospital remains and this is incorporated in
Holy Trinity Church in High Street. St Edmund,
King and Martyr, further south on Old Durham
Road, was intended for life-pensioners or bedes-
men who were admitted at the discretion of the
Master who was appointed by the bishop of
Durham. It was financed by rents from land in
Gateshead and Shotley Bridge and from the pro-
duce of coal seams underneath this land. In 1584
this coal was leased and three old people were
maintained in the hospital from the rent received
at a cost of 13/- a year each.

In 1611, St Edmund, King and Martyr, was
refounded as King James' Hospital as a result of
a petition to the King himself. The successive
Masters were the rectors of Gateshead who were
allowed one third of the hospital's income, which
cannot have been high, as during the latter part of
the seventeenth century and the eighteenth century, the fortunes of the hospital were at a very
low ebb. The cottages of the bedesmen had been
pulled down, and hens lived in the chapel. It was
reformed at the beginning of the nineteenth century by Dr Richard Prosser, the rector, whose
proposals included the re-erection of the cottages,
the supply to each of the inmates of a suit of
clothes each year and the provision of an adequate
supply of coal in the winter. The next Master was
the Reverend John Collinson who continued the

reforms and introduced another innovation, 'younger brethren', as well as the existing bedes-men. These 'younger brethren' had to be over 56 years of age, receiving less than £20 per annum and attending church regularly. Once accepted, they were given a pension, not exceeding £25 per annum.

From this time, the hospital prospered, and the chapel (St Edmund's) was rebuilt in 1810. In-creasing industrialisation enhanced the value of its land and the income rose accordingly so that by 1903 there were 46 'younger brethren' receiving £897 per annum between them. A new hospital has been opened on Sunderland Road at the time of writing.

A rate was levied by the parish to provide for the poor. A poor house was built in St Mary's churchyard and was in use in the seventeenth century but the largest portion of the money available was used to send paupers and vagrants back to their own parish in case they fell ill or died and caused even greater expense. At the beginning of the eighteenth century, Gateshead's trade was at a low ebb and the poor rate collected was raised to £148 per annum to help those un-employed. The parish gave financial assistance to those living at home as well as maintaining a poor house; in 1733, one hundred and forty-five were included in this category, at various rates per week, from 2d to 2/-.

Another parish poor house was acquired in 1750. In 1728 a Newcastle merchant, Thomas Powell, bequeathed all his wealth 'towards building an almshouse for poor men and women in Gateshead'. This almshouse was built in 1731 on the east side of the High Street and in 1750 the trustees of this bequest agreed with the parish overseers to convert the building into a poor house and later a workhouse. This change was illegal, against the terms of the bequest, but it was not questioned for almost a century, and after an enquiry, it became an almshouse once again in 1841.

Meanwhile, the poor rate had risen to £264 in 1757 and efforts were made to halt this unhappy trend. Assistance was withheld from those who refused to enter the poor house while from 1771 a man was paid £250 from which he had to feed and clothe the inhabitants of the poor house and pay any other expenses which arose. This system continued until 1809 when a permanent, salaried, Overseer of the Poor was appointed. The poor rate collected in 1810 amounted to £2,865 so committees were set up to report on the poor house and the out-relief payments which were now very large, the main recipients being widows and wives of men in the armed forces.

In 1813 rules were laid down to reorganise the poor house which show something of the life 'inside'. The main aim appears to be cleanliness— clean blankets every 6 months, clean sheets every

3 weeks and a daily wash for the inmates. The poor rate was still rising and those receiving assistance were put to work levelling High Street, probably in the hope that this would deter others from seeking relief.

An Act of 1819 changed the administration of the Poor Law. A Select Vestry was chosen by ratepayers and included many people from the four-and-twenty. One of its duties was to examine all applicants for relief, a kind of means test, and as a result the poor rate fell from £4,500 in 1820 to £3,040 in 1822, although mild weather and cheap food were factors which affected the number of applicants. The poor rate was held steady until 1831 when removals of vagrants to Scotland and Ireland, a cholera epidemic and then in 1832 a miners' strike placed an intolerable burden on Gateshead causing a sudden rise to £4,709.

A further Act, the Poor Law Amendment Act of 1834 established Poor Law Unions (neighbouring parishes grouped together) which were operated by Boards of Guardians. The first meeting of the Gateshead Board took place on 14 December 1836, in Gateshead. The area covered was approximately the same as the new Gateshead Metropolitan District Council area, extending to Chopwell, Crawcrook and Heworth. This Board of Guardians remained in power until 1930. The Guardians resolved to build a new workhouse which would be better suited to the purpose and

eventually decided on a site off Coatsworth Road,
now Woodbine Street, in the then fashionable
suburb of Bensham: a healthy site was necessary
for the recovery of the sick. This new building
was opened in July 1841 with accommodation
for 276 inmates. Powell's Almshouses reverted to
their original purpose. They were finally demolished in 1947 and new homes for the almspeople
were built in Cross Keys Lane in 1962.

Gateshead's increasing population meant larger
numbers of inmates in the workhouse. A new
workhouse was first suggested in 1863 but it was
June 1890 before High Teams Workhouse was
occupied. The Guardians had trouble in finding
a suitable site. Heworth, Low Fell, Saltwell and
Whickham were all discussed but eventually High
Teams Farm was bought in 1885, the un-
employed were used to level the area and to make
bricks, and building began. The parts of the farm
not used for the workhouse were leased and then
sold for house building, the Guardians making
money to ease the rates by inserting restrictive
covenants against the sale of alcohol into the legal
transactions (this meant public houses could not
be built) and then withdrawing the covenants at a
high price.

When one thinks of workhouses today, one
associates them with poor living conditions, inadequate food and clothing, harsh masters and
matrons, very little education for children and

no means of enjoyment for the inmates. In Gateshead there were complaints, frequently about the food, although only the best was ordered, and on one occasion, the master and matron were found to be locking up troublesome inmates in the mortuary! The inmates were expected to work, the women performed domestic duties while the men worked on the High Team farm or broke stones for the roads. Although some nurses appointed in the early days of the Guardians were inclined to alcoholism, the standard improved later and generally the staff appear to have done their best to improve life for the inmates. When one matron, Mrs Penrose, died in 1886, the Board of Guardians paid tribute to her: 'To the aged inmates she was a comforting counsellor, while in her, each child found a parent.'

Children were a special problem, they had to be educated and attempts were made to rid them of the workhouse stigma. Classes were held within the workhouse for girls (1841) and boys (1851). Teaching methods improved and in 1895 all the children attended Brighton Avenue Board School. Footballs and the use of a playing field were provided. Other attempts to improve the way of life of the children were emigration to Canada, carefully supervised apprenticeships and boarding-out of children to foster parents. This latter scheme was not successful as those interested quickly realised that it was not a cheap way to acquire a

domestic servant. Trips to Tynemouth and pantomimes in Newcastle and Gateshead theatres were
arranged. After 1869, modest attempts were made
to vary their clothes as the uniform branded a
child as a workhouse inmate.

Eventually, cottage homes were opened in 1901
at Shotley Bridge, the first in the North-East. Six
cottages provided for 120 boys and 90 girls and
at first met with some hostility from local residents
(this had been a problem in selecting a site for
the workhouse itself) but continued in use until
1930 when they were handed over to Durham
County Council.

One group of inmates in the workhouse received
very little sympathy, the tramps and vagrants who
slept in the casual ward of the workhouse. They
were a problem from the mid-nineteenth century
and several times suggestions were put forward
that the vagrant wards be demolished. On one
night in January 1865, twenty-three people slept
on the stone floor of a room 12 feet square! Later
on, in the 1890s, attempts were made to distin-
guish between those who had left home in search
of work, and vagrants who knew no other way of
life. In 1901 it came to light that the master of
Newcastle Workhouse was turning away vagrants
and advising them to come to Gateshead! This
practice was discontinued after complaints by
Gateshead Guardians.

The miners' strike in 1926 brought acute financial embarrassment to Gateshead Guardians as it did to most other Boards in mining areas. At the end of the year, Gateshead's debt stood at £250,000 and they had to borrow to pay necessary bills. The mass unemployment and the economic problems of this period were the causes of the breakdown in administration of the Poor Law. The Local Government Act of 1929 abolished Boards of Guardians and transferred their functions to county borough and county councils.

The High Teams Institution continued as before but in August 1948, the name was changed to Fountain View and the internal organisation was reformed, the old workhouse furniture was sold and modern styles substituted while the drab paintwork gave way to bright, cheerful colours. As time went on, the council realised that Fountain View was inadequate for its purpose—it now catered for old people. The residents were transferred to newly-built old people's homes such as Alderwood and Cedarwood and the old workhouse was demolished in 1969. Gateshead was a pioneer in this field in the North-East.

Since the Second World War, Gateshead Corporation has taken maximum advantage of the relevant Acts of Parliament to become a leader in the provision of social services to all sections of the community. Recent innovations include a club for the handicapped, opened in April 1972 by

Lord Shinwell, and the provision of telephones
for the housebound.

Health

Until the twentieth century Gateshead was an unpleasant place in which to live from the health
point of view. In medieval times public health
services were non-existent and the policy of isolation was used when serious illness or plagues were
present in the town. Temporary huts were built
at Bensham for this purpose but there was no
preventive action. During the plagues of the seventeenth century, the market or butter cross at
Ravensworth was used as a place to deposit goods
and money. Country people, unaffected by the
plague, left food around the base of the cross
and town dwellers took it and left money in ex-
change. Apparently this was later disinfected in
vinegar!

Early Gateshead was a perfect breeding ground
for disease of all kinds. The houses were packed
close together, lodging houses and tenements were
crowded, there were insufficient drains, refuse and
sewage were thrown into the streets and several
unpleasant trades, such as slaughtering and glue
making were carried on close to houses. Cholera
first appeared in Gateshead in December 1831,
the first victim being 'a female rag-gatherer of
depraved habits'. The epidemic lasted a year,
resulting in 234 deaths, and was the impetus in

the opening of the Dispensary in 1832. The Dispensary did not alleviate the problem as sufficient money was not available, those who paid rates did not live in the squalid parts of the town and did not suffer from the epidemics as much as the poor lower classes.

A police report in 1835 on lodging houses illustrated the problem: 'There were 34 people in one house mostly Irish, including one dead child.' Another report on Gateshead in 1843 showed that while the population was 38,747 only 110 houses had a direct water supply. Pipewellgate was 300 yards long, the thoroughfare was 8 feet wide and the population was 2,040. In 1849 cholera broke out for a second time, the disease was thought to have been brought by a tramp from Edinburgh who stayed at Williams' lodging house where the 24 'guests' slept two to a bed! This epidemic again lasted for one year. An enquiry by the General Board of Health in 1849 described the squalor of some parts of the town which in some cases was unbelievable. The third and last outbreak occurred in 1853 but, typhus, brought by Irish immigrants, was often present. The Borough Surveyor thought that the only way to free the town of such diseases was to demolish Pipewellgate and Hillgate. His prayers were partly answered in 1854 when the Great Fire destroyed most of the latter but the former was not completely levelled until the 1930s.

A sanitary inspector and part-time medical officer of health were appointed in 1866 and 1873 respectively but the high mortality rate was the cause of an enquiry by the local government board inspector, Dr Barry, in 1884. The lodging houses had improved since the 1850s but the tenements were very bad and the slaughter-houses were disgusting. Barry praised the public baths in Oakwellgate built in 1855 (the building still stands, 1974) and the isolation hospital at Sheriff Hill, despite its deficiences. However, the baths were not used to capacity due to the high charges. The death rate in some parts of the town was very high; in Oakwellgate it was 36.5 per 1000 whereas the national average was 19.3.

In 1884 a full-time medical officer of health, a Dr Robinson, was appointed at a salary of £400, the improvements gained impetus, and the epidemics began to die out. The last smallpox outbreak ended in 1905, but children's diseases such as measles and whooping cough still had a strong hold and the infant mortality rate was high. The main problem was that the population was so poor that the town could not support sufficient doctors to provide an adequate health service. Diphtheria, scarlet fever and tuberculosis remained a danger until the 1940s.

Sewers were built to drain the now expanding town. A water carriage system to replace the ash-pits had been suggested in 1898 but it was not until a government grant was available in 1925 that the work was undertaken and 18,706 houses were converted within two years. Alderman P. S. Hancock deserves much of the credit for this improvement as he campaigned energetically for this cause and in fact was awarded the O.B.E. for his work in public health. In the 1920s, the Gateshead population reached its peak, so the influx of those needing houses decreased from this date. The Tyne Bridge was built at this time with the result that the worst slums were cleared to make way for the approaches and supports for the bridge. Inspection improved the quality of food shops and competent municipal health services began to operate, centred on Greenesfield House, which has been the centre of corporation health activities from 1920.

Gateshead lacked hospital accommodation. Sheriff Hill Isolation Hospital was extended in 1904, while Saltwell Hall was also used at a hospital for infectious diseases for a time. Whinney House was another stately home which was converted to this purpose. Finance was not available for new building until 1936 and the Queen Elizabeth Hospital was begun at Sheriff Hill in 1938. Unfortunately, the Second World War delayed the completion of this building and the hospital wards of the workhouse were taken over. This later became Bensham General Hospital.

The chapel of St. Edmund's Hospital in 1774, now the southern portion of Holy Trinity Church

OLD NEWCASTLE OLD BRIDGE OVER TYNE in 1770   № 7

The medieval Tyne bridge, destroyed by floods in 1771

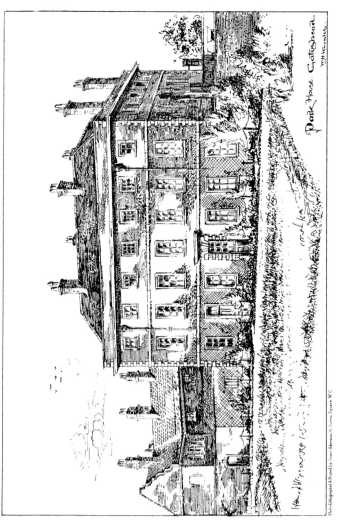

Park House, Gateshead.
W.H. Knowles.

Photo-Lithographed & Printed by James Akerman, 6 Queen Square W.C.

Park House, designed by James Gibbs for Henry Ellison, and built 1730-33. Drawn by
W. H. Knowles in about 1889

Redheugh Hall

REDHEUGH HOUSE.

Ellison Square. Built about 1851 on garden ground between Ellison Street and Nelson Street

The Goat Inn, Bottle Bank, 1924

Friar's Goose and East Gateshead Riverside Park, 1972

(Courtesy of Turners (Photography) Ltd.)

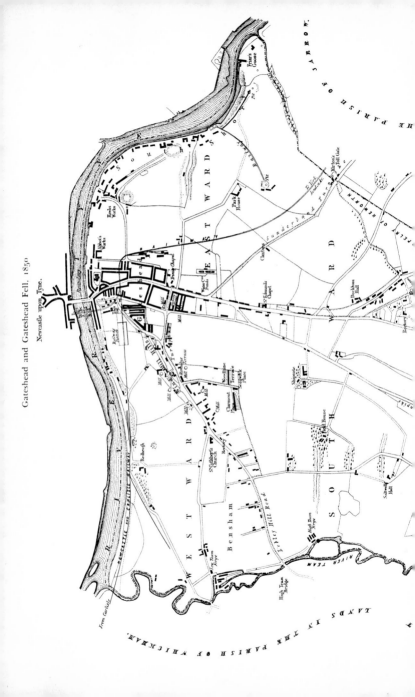

Gateshead and Gateshead Fell. 1850

Newcastle upon Tyne.

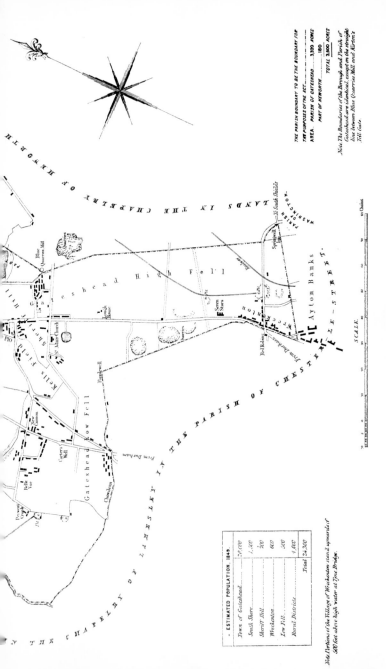

Gateshead and Gateshead Fell, 1850

The riverfront, Pipewellgate, about 1880. The Fountain Inn at centre

Dryden's farm at Shipcote, 1935

Powell's Court and Almshouses, High Street, 1924

High Street, looking north, about 1906

Steam-hauled tramcar, High Street, 1900

Pipewellgate, looking east, June 1886

Low Fell from the site of Dryden Senior High School, about 1932

The Queen Elizabeth Hospital was officially opened on 18 March 1948.

St Mary's Hospital at Stannington serves the town's present needs for a mental hospital. Previously, mentally ill patients were catered for at private asylums situated at Wrekenton (1825-55), Sheriff Hill (1817-60) and Bensham (1799-1868). Part of the latter building can still be seen on Sidney Grove.

Gateshead Council sent patients to an asylum owned by Durham County Council from 1856 but this agreement was ended in 1912. An estate was bought at Stannington for £9,221 and the hospital was opened in 1914.

Housing

Until the mid-nineteenth century, the area now covered by Gateshead was essentially rural in character. The population was centred on the river and the steep banks above. Pipewellgate and Hillgate had been rebuilt in the eighteenth century while High Street was 'one continued line of buildings of various and irregular appearance'. Little building had been done since 1801 and by 1831 the population had doubled to 15,177. This was the start of Gateshead's housing problem, as insufficient dwellings were constructed to keep pace with demand. There were crowded slums behind the main streets, approached by narrow alleyways which sometimes served as open drains.

The richer people moved away from the town centre to Low Fell and Bensham where select houses such as Claremont Place (1819-24) were built and their large town houses were tenemented: even cellars were let to the poorer classes. As late as 1932 the roof of one such house at 13 Mulgrave Terrace fell in and 54 people were made homeless!

Further select houses such as Walker Terrace and Regent Terrace were built in the mid-nineteenth century and when part of the Shipcote estate was sold for working-class dwellings, it was stipulated that the houses facing Regent Terrace (Queens Terrace) were to be of better quality so that Regent Terrace would not be devalued by the presence of poorer houses. House building increased with estates at Mount Pleasant, and Windmill Hills (the northern Coatsworth Road area) developed from 1850. During the 1860s houses were built from the Hills down to St Cuthbert's Road. In 1865 came the break-up of the large estates in the town and the start of construction of large houses for wealthy industrialists at Low Fell (Ashfield, Enfield) and Saltwell (Ferndene). Large areas of Shipcote, Redheugh, Teams and Sunderland Road were built over up to 1875 when there was a temporary halt. The houses were mostly of the terraced flat variety, developed by tradesmen of Gateshead and occupied by skilled workers; the labourers still

lived in the slums of the town centre. A second
wave of building began in 1885 and the inhabitants of the earlier type of flat moved to the new
variety. The older flats were in turn taken over
by the poorer classes.

The town centre slums were degenerating even
further. The authorities, like their predecessors
throughout the nineteenth century, were not
really aware of the shocking conditions in which
people lived. Moves to encourage the council to
build houses in 1899 were defeated. One alderman, as if explaining the situation said, 'dirty
people make dirty houses'.

There was still a shortage of good houses, and
as the population had increased and the First
World War had halted most of the building in
the town, the situation became even worse, with
one in three people living in overcrowded conditions. After the war the council yielded to local
demands and began to build houses for rent, the
first council houses were built at Carr Hill and
Sheriff Hill in the early 1920s. Council house
building progressed, but there was still a shortage
of houses as very successful slum clearance in the
1930s made increasing demands on the building
programme. Council houses were built in all parts
of the town and by 1954 there was a desperate
shortage of land.

In 1948 a report on this problem suggested a
new town of 80,000, eight miles west of Gateshead,

to be called Barlow, but the idea received little
or no support. The answer to the housing problem
was seen in multi-storey blocks, usually built on the
old slum areas, although the existence of old
mineworkings limited available sites in the town,
although special foundations can alleviate this
problem. The first block of flats on Tyneside was
that completed at Barn Close in 1955. Others
followed; Regent Court 1958, Bensham 1962 and
Chandless 1962/3. These large blocks did not
solve the social problems and the 'village' concept
has been tried at Redheugh with popular Clasper
Village and St Cuthbert's Village.

Despite the large waiting list for council houses,
Gateshead Council's record of house building is
second to none: during the years 1946-70 the
number of houses built totalled 10,686, this works
out as an average of almost two houses per working
day!

Leisure

How the people of Gateshead spent their leisure
time varied according to their social status and
income. Letters in the Cotesworth and Ellison
family papers in Gateshead Central Library show
the hobbies and pursuits of the upper and wealthy
classes. As might be expected, hunting and horse-
riding occupied a lot of their time together with
breeding suitable dogs. Horses were highly
prized possessions as they were the best means of

land transport. Cock-fighting was enjoyed late into
the eighteenth century but it was dying out as a
common sport although there are advertisements in
local newspapers for cockpits at public houses in
Gateshead in the 1770s. They also indulged in
more gentle pursuits. The ladies had their sew-
ing and the gentlemen looked after the garden;
they only supervised, of course; gardeners were
employed to do the hard work. Apricots were
grown in the garden of Park House, obviously
the climate was rather better than it is today!
When in London, the opera and theatre were
excellent diversions and reading helped pass the
time at home. Newspapers kept them up to date
with world events while the latest plays and
poetry were read in place of the novels which are
taken for granted today.

The poorer people had very little leisure time.
Very long hours were common as late as 1890
when chemical workers still worked a 72-hour,
six-day week. Sunday was the only free day. As
the ordinary worker could not afford to spend a
lot on recreation, his hobbies were very simple.
The country lanes which led from Gateshead were
ideal for a pleasant stroll in the fresh air, away
from the fumes of chemical works or dirt of coal
mines.

There were activities common to all classes.
Hunting was a common interest, although when
the poor took an occasional rabbit it was called

poaching. Gamekeepers were employed more as a deterrent to poachers than to conserve and increase the supply of game birds. The public houses were popular with all classes of people as they provided meeting places as well as drinking places. They became the centre of social life of the town.

During the nineteenth century, Durham and Northumberland were at the top of drunkenness leagues, and societies, such as the Rechabites and Bands of Hope, were formed to combat this problem. Temperance halls were set up but in 1846 there were reported to be 73 adult teetotallers in Gateshead along with 49 juveniles, and only 4 ministers! Of course, the rest of the population were not alcoholics but they were not members of the temperance movement. Strangely enough, Wesleyan Methodists would not allow teetotal movements the use of their rooms but this rule was ignored in Gateshead. 'The Temperance Committee have the use of the schoolroom for 2/6 per night, that they refrain from abusive language, that on no occasion whatever are they to stand upon the furniture.' Obviously, they did not need alcohol to make them unruly!

Drunkenness increased, but so did the population. In 1851 one in every 168 people of Gateshead was convicted of drunkenness, but in all fairness it was pointed out that 'the Gatesiders, ... are not disorderly in their cups, but go pretty quietly

along the streets when drunk!' Large numbers of
immigrants, especially the Irish and Scots, may have
contributed to this problem. One supporter of
temperance was George Lucas who wrote pam-
phlets pointing out that the 170 public houses in
the 1860s earned their proprietors approximately
£80,000 per year. The population of Gateshead
was only 35,000 at this time.

One such pamphlet caused a rather humorous
situation. Lucas proposed to lecture on a Gateshead
magistrate who had recently died, it was said, of
alcoholism. The nephew of the deceased, resented
the criticism of his uncle and attacked Lucas with
a whip. The meeting did not take place as the
police could not guarantee to keep the peace,
rumour had it that a mob had been offered free
beer by a publican to break up the lecture and
that three men were seen near the Temperance
Hall in Ellison Square 'seeking the main gas pipe'.

The working men's clubs began to appear in
London in the 1860s. The earliest recorded in
Gateshead were temperance clubs—this was not an
uncommon phenomenon, as the main object of
these clubs was mental and moral improvement.
The boom in working men's clubs came during the
years 1900-14, when about 17 were formed in
Gateshead, including some which are still in
existence; Redheugh Social, Teams and District,
Saltwell Social, and High Fell. Others were short-
lived as enthusiasm of the members waned. Some,

like the Empire Workmen's Club in Southend
Terrace, lost their licence for too many cases of
drunkenness amongst the members. After the First
World War a second group of clubs opened and the
public houses introduced various sports to regain
some of the business lost to the clubs. From about
1905, quoits was played in wooden sheds behind
pubs such as the Patent Hammer, the Fountain
Inn and the Plough at Deckham. The game was
very popular for some time but interest diminished
so that by 1930 not a single shed was in use.

Billiards was formerly an aristocratic pursuit but
was introduced into some pubs, the Beehive,
Arthur Street; the Star, Forster Street and the
Shakespeare, Deckham by 1900. Purpose-built
halls were opened in Corporation buildings, High
Street (1906), the Crown, Sunderland Road (1912)
and at Coatsworth Road and Low Fell. These dis-
placed the pub billiard rooms and were themselves closed by 1957.

As the nineteenth century progressed, the working classes had more free time as working hours
decreased. It was at this time that Gateshead
acquired two public parks, Windmill Hills and
Saltwell Park. The Windmill Hills had been a
favourite place for meetings, concerts, sports and
Whitsun hoppings for many years, but in 1861 it
was handed over to the council by the borough-
holders as the first public park in Gateshead. The
local newspaper had campaigned for such a park,

expressing a general public need for such a facility. On the actual transfer day, there was a general holiday, and the factories closed to allow the ordinary workmen to witness the ceremony. Although this was a popular park, it was eclipsed by the opening of Saltwell Park in 1876. This was bought for £32,000 from William Wailes, who had had Saltwell Towers built, and a further £11,000 was spent on landscaping, including the artificial lake which was made in 1880. Since then all the town's social activities centred on the park; Coronation celebrations have been held there, activities were organised for 'Holidays at Home' during the Second World War, the town festival takes place each July and now there are some 'hoppings' in August. A new part at East Gateshead is being developed from former industrial wasteland but Saltwell will still hold the unofficial title of the 'best park in the North-East' for many years to come.

The theatre, music hall and cinema were very popular pastimes but now this part of the entertainment industry is a shadow of its former self; having been overtaken by television. Music halls were first held in pubs but shows became too large and separate premises were taken. The first in Gateshead was the Alexandra at the corner of Oakwellgate Chare and High Street, opened on 14 November 1870. The acts on the first bill included a female impersonator and clog dancers, but the theatre closed the following year after an 'unseemly performance'. The building was later used by the Salvation Army and the Baptists. The next music hall was in a large public house in Bottle Bank and seated 400 people. Known as the People's Music Hall, it had a short life from 1874-80. The owner of the 'Peoples' was a George Handyside, who later built the Handyside Arcade in Newcastle. He tried to establish another hall at Pleasant Row but residents of the area petitioned against his plans and a theatre licence was withheld. Music halls were socially unacceptable in those days.

The first theatres in the town were travelling troupes, playing wherever an audience could be gathered, sometimes in Methuen's Long Room on High Street, sometimes at the New Cannon at Low Fell. A temporary theatre was set up in Oakwellgate and put on pantomimes as well as travelling players and works of local playwright Isaac Tucker, a brass founder. Unfortunately, his first dramatic effort in 1845 produced roars of laughter and applause instead of the more genteel appreciation which he had hoped for.

The first permanent theatre was the Queens on High Street. The building had a chequered history as a chapel (1815), music hall, boxing hall, Salvation Army hall (1882), Royal Theatre (1887), the Queens (1894), and the New Hippodrome Cinema (1919). It was badly damaged by fire in

1922 and a Woolworth store was built on the site. A tragedy occurred in 1891 when seven children were crushed to death during a scramble to escape after a false fire alarm.

The most luxurious theatre in Gateshead was the Metropole, at the corner of High Street and Jackson Street, opened on 28 September 1896, by Weldon Watts, former owner of the Queens. The Metropole had a marble staircase, brass handrails, and a ceiling of elaborate plasterwork. Touring companies provided most of the plays and as these declined in number, the building became the Scala Cinema in 1919. As befitted the splendour of the building, the changeover was carried out in a grand manner. A large orchestra and later a £3,000 organ played music for the silent films.

The first permanent cinema was the Askew, opened in 1909. Moving pictures had been shown by travelling showmen and shopkeepers converted their premises to cash in on what proved to be a profitable sideline. The Askew was in fact one of the latter group and was generally known as 'Horns'. Other early cinemas were the Ravensworth, nicknamed 'the Rats', opened in 1909, Black's Palace (1909), Empress Electric Theatre ('Loppy Lloyds', 1910) and the Shipcote (1911). 'Loppy Lloyds' was always the cheapest in town. During the harsh depression years, admission cost 1d, 2d or 3d, while matinees cost three jam jars. The 1930s saw another spate of new cinemas.

Black's Regal, now the Odeon, was opened by no
less a star than Gracie Fields in 1937 and by 1950
there were fifteen cinemas in Gateshead but this
was the peak year. Television and bingo were the
cause of many closures, although the Essoldo and
Ritz were demolished to make way for the Gateshead Highway. Now only two remain, the Odeon
and the recently opened Classic which has brought
the three in one cinema concept to the town.

Today, most people think of competitive rowing
in terms of the university boat race, but in the
latter part of the nineteenth century, rowing was a
popular spectator sport and the North-East produced several well-known oarsmen such as Ren-
forth of Gateshead, Clasper of Dunston and
Chambers from Byker. These men were cham-
pions and their popularity can be gauged by the
fact that their funerals were attended by many
thousands. Robert Cooper from Redheugh was
said to be one of the most scientific scullers on
the Tyne, but skill was not enough and he did
not win a major race. The prizes were considerable, Clasper was awarded £200 for one race in
1858 while Chambers won £400 for a day's work
in 1864. Spectators lined the banks of the river
to cheer on their favourites and spent such money
as they had betting on the rival oarsmen.

The British national sport is football and most
towns have a football league side. Gateshead is
one of the few which does not. In fact, the last

Gateshead A.F.C. has recently closed down following financial difficulties. Teams from Gateshead had existed from about 1880, but the first Gateshead A.F.C. was formed in 1913, playing at grounds at Old Ford and the Shuttles. They played against teams from Shildon, Houghton, Newcastle Reserves and Sunderland Reserves in the North Eastern League. It is not generally realised that the second Gateshead A.F.C. was originally a South Shields team which changed its name and ground after severe financial difficulties. This team's first game against Doncaster attracted a crowd of 15,545 on 30 August 1930, but it declined in the following years. Falling receipts were partially relieved by a greyhound track in the stadium and Hughie Gallagher signed for the club with the result of improved performances from 1938-45 and interest in the town was revived. Unfortunately, the standard of play fell again and during the 1950/51 season gates fell from 11,000 to 2,000.

There were brief moments of glory, however. In 1953 Gateshead reached the sixth round of the F.A. Cup, people queued at the Town Hall for tickets and cup fever hit the town. The cup tie was played against Bolton who won 1—0. In 1955 Tottenham Hotspur came to Gateshead to compete in the same competition and 18,840 people turned out to see their team defeated 2—0. Gateshead's first season in the Fourth Division was their last. They suffered several heavy defeats and applied unsuccessfully for re-election. The official reason for their exclusion from the football league was given as poor gates, but the real reason was either the rumoured Yorkshire/Lancashire conspiracy, or the existence of a greyhound racing track within the ground.

The club joined the Northern Premier League, then the Wearside League in 1970 and then the Midland League but in August 1973 closed down. Almost immediately, another team, Gateshead Town was formed to play in the Northern Combination League, and recently (January 1974) there have been reports that another South Shields A.F.C. will move to Gateshead Youth Sports Stadium.

CHAPTER SIX

INDUSTRY

Coal Mining

Tyneside is always associated with industry, especially coal which has been mined here for hundreds of years. Coal mining arrived in Gateshead rather later than in the rest of County Durham; the first recorded mention being in 1344, although coal was probably mined before this. As explained in earlier chapters, medieval Gateshead was the property of the bishops of Durham and was linked with another ecclesiastical manor, Whickham, in leases for coal mining. The pits were relatively shallow and all the work was done by hand, but as time went on more and more coal was produced until the mid-sixteenth century when Gateshead and Whickham contained the most productive coalfields in the world. 400,000 tons were shipped from the Tyne in 1625 as compared with 35,000 tons in 1565. Only one Gateshead family appears to have made a fortune in this trade, the appropriately named Cole family. As well as leasing and working their own mines, they were money lenders and many of the Newcastle coal owners were in debt to them.

As could be expected, Gateshead at this time was scarred by coal mines and although no traces can be seen on the surface today, the town rests on a maze of galleries and shafts which occasionally make their presence known by sudden subsidence.

Towards the end of the seventeenth century, the easily won coal seams were largely worked out and the industry moved further from the river in search of fresh reserves at Tanfield and Stella. However, small groups of men continued to work the outcrops which larger concerns would have found uneconomic. The number of these smaller pits grew, and in 1720 there were 156 on the Shipcote Estate alone!

Coal was mined near to water transportation facilities as land transport was confined to the horse on very poor or non-existent roads. Packhorses were used to carry the coal to the staiths and later horses or oxen pulled large heavy wagons known as wains down to the river. The scale of the industry can be gauged by the fact that in Whickham 700 of these wains were in daily use. Wagonways, used from the mid-seventeenth century, were really a means of giving the horse-drawn wain a smoother passage. Wagonways in Gateshead included the Ravensworth, which ran down the west of the Team Valley to Dunston, Gateshead Fell from the Fell to Redheugh, but later to the

South Shore, crossing the Old Durham Road, just
north of King James's Hospital and from Sheriff
Hill to the Engine pit at Low Fell. After the inven-
tion and improvement of the steam pumping
engine, deeper seams could be worked as the water
(if present), could be drawn off. In 1765 such an
engine cost £1000. Park Colliery and Tyne Main
Colliery at Friars' Goose had these engines, the
latter had the most powerful on the Tyne, pro-
ducing about 180 horsepower and capable of
pumping 1,444,800 gallons of water per day, ten
times the capacity of Shipcote Baths. Part of the
remains of the engine house can still be seen today
in East Gateshead riverside park.

Coal mining continued at a few larger pits within the town, at Redheugh, Oakwellgate and near
the junction of High Street and Sunderland Road.
The last colliery to close was at Redheugh between
Lower Cuthbert Street and Morrison Street off
Askew Road. Sunk in 1872, it produced 120,000
tons of coal per annum in the 1890s and gave
employment to about 420 men and boys but became unproductive and closed in 1927.

Quarries

Another very old industry was quarrying which
left many workings scattered throughout Gateshead, especially the Fell, although there were
several near the town itself, at Barns Close, Wylam
Street, behind Pleasant Row (High Street) and

on Bensham Bank opposite Bloomfield Terrace. These were used for the extensive housebuilding programmes of the nineteenth century but were later filled in and built over themselves.

In the eighteenth century the trade was largely concerned with grindstones, many of which were exported. The quarrymen themselves were a constant source of trouble to their landlord, the lord of the manor. Frequently they did not pay their rent and dumped rubbish and spoil at random and generally 'they followed their work without taking notice of anybody'. One lord of the manor was advised thus: 'If you do not make a publicke example of some of those fellowes they'll ride on your shoulders as long as you live.'

As time went on the grindstone trade decreased and the emphasis was placed on the quarrying of building stone, especially during the rebuilding of central Newcastle in the 1830s. The number of men employed in this trade was never large, only 75 in Gateshead and the Fell in 1839, one of the boom periods for this trade.

Milling

From medieval times Gateshead had been a centre for milling corn. Windmills were mentioned as early as 1183 in the Boldon Book while watermills were built in the fourteenth century. From the relatively large number of mills, Gateshead seems to have been a centre for this kind of industry:

in 1709 there were eleven of both kinds at work. Towards the end of the eighteenth century some surviving mills were converted to the new form of power, steam, although this method had its drawbacks as mills were notorious fire risks.

As may be deduced, most of the mills were to be found on Windmill Hills although there were others in Hillgate, High Street, Jackson Street, Bensham and Carr Hill. During the nineteenth century, the windmills fell into disuse or were used for other purposes such as storehouses, tenement dwellings and, in one case, a summer cottage! The last working mill in the town stood at the corner of Jackson Street and West Street and worked until the 1890s. The Old Mill Inn and later the Co-operative Store were built on the site. The last mill on Windmill Hills was demolished in July 1927 but a mill at Carr Hill survived as a derelict shell until 1964.

Pottery

The pottery industry is a very old trade, older than coal mining (and was carried out on a world wide basis, people needed utensils and plates, no matter what period of history they lived in). The early pottery industry in Gateshead is still the subject of research, but as early as the fourteenth century clay was brought from Heworth in large quantities to be worked in kilns in the town. One such kiln was uncovered, although greatly damaged, on the

site of the Ritz cinema during the construction
of the Gateshead Highway.

There then appears to have been a decline in
this industry and potteries were not worked again
in Gateshead until the eighteenth century. There
were small potteries at the South Shore and later
at Bensham, Pipewellgate and Low Teams, but
the main centres were at Carr Hill and Sheriff
Hill. John Warburton, probably a native of
Staffordshire, opened a pottery at Newcastle and
in 1740 moved the manufacturing side of the
business to Carr Hill. He is said to have been the
first to introduce white earthenware into the
district. Warburton died in 1795 and the business
was carried on by his son and then his widow
until 1817 when the white ware was discontinued.
From 1817 the pottery had a variety of owners, the
last being Thomas Patterson of Sheriff Hill pottery,
until it closed in 1893. The building was demolished in 1932. The Old Brown Jug public house
serves as a reminder of the trade once practised
nearby.

Paul Jackson established the Sheriff Hill pottery
in 1771 at the corner of Pottersway and Old
Durham Road. Members of the Jackson family
were partners in the business until 1837 when
Thomas Patterson took over. By 1839 there were
50 employees, many of whom lived in a row of
cottages adjoining the Old Cannon Inn. This
pottery closed in 1909 and the buildings were

demolished in the 1920s to make way for council houses.

Engineering

The earliest instance of metal manufacture in Gateshead was 1528 when attempts were made to smelt Weardale lead and extract silver on the instruction of Thomas Wolsey, then Bishop of Durham. The experiment was a failure and the furnace far from efficient, molten metal leaked out 'at every side'. The next venture was more successful. In 1721, William Cotesworth, lord of the manor, leased an iron and brass foundry at Pipewellgate to Isaac Cookson. This business prospered and lasted until the early 1850s when the foundry closed and the premises were used to refine antimony.

The famous ironmaster, Sir Ambrose Crowley, established factories in old water mills at High and Low Teams in 1735 as extensions to his premises at Swalwell and Winlaton. Nails, locks, spades and general iron products were made there but the workforce was relatively small when compared with the more famous premises on the Derwent. The firm declined at the end of the eighteenth century but the Gateshead factories were in use until 1860. Low Team forge was afterwards used as a paper mill while High Team forge was incorporated in the farm buildings of the Teams estate.

The best known heavy engineering firm of old
Gateshead was, of course, Hawks, Crawshay &
Sons. The firm was started in 1748 by William
Hawks at New Greenwich at the South Shore.
Hawks had been a foreman blacksmith at Crowley's
works and he named his first factory after Crowley's old premises at Greenwich on the Thames.
William Hawks II took control of the firm in 1775
and expanded his premises and trade, foundries
were bought and steam introduced. By 1801 the
firm produced several kinds of ordnance, anchors,
chains, bolts, spades and many other metal products. Government contracts were taken over from
the declining firm of Crowley and the stage was
set for a successful period of trade, helped by the
Napoleonic wars and therefore a constant demand
for weapons. The new premises were known as
New Deptford and New Woolwich, built to the
west of the older works. (Hawks' had warehouses
on the Thames at these places.) By the end of the
eighteenth century this by now prosperous concern had its own ships to transport its goods.

In 1839, Hawks' employed approximately 800
men and boys. Skilled tradesmen earned 22 shillings per week while labourers were paid 2 shillings
per day. An investigation was made into the working conditions of children in the works in 1842;
the following example illustrates the hard life
which these children led. One twelve-year-old boy
had already worked at Hawks' factory for 3

years. His hours were 6.00 a.m. to 6.00 p.m. (summer, 1½ hours, for meals), and 6.00 a.m. to 5.00 p.m. (winter, ¾ hr. for meals). On Saturdays work ended at 4.00 p.m. This particular boy was paid *4/- per week* for carrying iron to furnaces and his ambition was to be apprenticed as a chainmaker at a wage of 6/- per week. The only holidays were 2 days at Christmas and 2 half days at Easter and Whitsuntide. As at Crowley's, the employees of Hawks had certain benefits; schools for workers and their children, houses provided by the firm and a code of rules with fines for swearing, betting and drinking. Despite the hard work, very low wages and long hours (all were typical of the period), 'Haaks' men' were apparently contented workers.

The firm began to design and build many different products ranging from paddle steamers to dredgers and from bridges to lighthouses! Everyone has heard of the High Level Bridge, built by Hawks' 1846-49, but they also constructed iron bridges as far afield as Constantinople and India. However impressive these achievements may sound, they were the cause of the closure of the company, coupled with the incompetence of George Crawshay, a partner in the firm. Specialist manufacturers expanded and were more successful than a firm such as Hawks which tried to make everything; the Armstrong works at Elswick were divided into specialist departments while William Galloway, the nail manufacturer, became a force to be reckoned with in that branch of the iron trade.

Hawks, Crawshay and Sons (the firm had many changes of name and this was the last) closed suddenly in September 1889, but every creditor was paid in full and today this name remains a proud reminder of Gateshead's industrial past.

John Abbot & Co. was the only other Gateshead engineering firm to approach the size of Hawks and met a similar fate. From a small firm which had existed for some years, Abbot's grew in the 1820s and 1830s until in 1841, 640 men and boys were employed in factories to the east of Oakwellgate known as Park Works. The output diversified considerably until they produced everything from tin tacks to railway engines, but the decline was as fast as the growth and the firm went into liquidation in 1909.

William Galloway was a nail manufacturer with premises at the end of Sunderland Road, established in the late 1850s. His firm only employed about 25 to 50 people by 1900, many of them women, but, nevertheless, it took business from the giants of Hawks and Abbot. One interesting aspect of this business is the fact that it held an agency for French and American steam cars. Galloway's moved to Blaydon in 1952 and was taken over by the industrial giant G.K.N. in 1965.

Today many do not realise that Gateshead was

a railway town with workshops employing 3,300 men in 1909, but the first engine was seen in Gateshead more than one hundred years before this. John Winfield, who had a foundry in Pipewellgate, became an agent for Richard Trevethick's railway engine and by May 1805 a prototype was built in the town. It was never used outside, its only movements were on a short track within the foundry. Thomas Waters of Gateshead acquired the agency and built another engine in 1813. These were small scale operations, but the next locomotive builder, Coulthard and Co. of Oakwellgate, was a bigger concern, actually building engines for use by railway companies during the years 1839-65. The premises were taken over by Black, Hawthorn and Co., an even bigger firm who manufactured engines for ships and steam trams as well as railways. In 1889 there were about 1,000 employees but the business went into liquidation in 1896.

The cause of the decline of Coulthard's and Black, Hawthorn's was the steady expansion of the Greenesfield workshops by the North Eastern Railway Company, the greatest employer of labour in Gateshead in 1900, which built and repaired railway locomotives. Unfortunately, the site at Greenesfield was rather small and the N.E.R. decided to transfer the engine building part of the works to Darlington in 1909 and in 1932 the rest of the works were closed. Both these dates represented heavy blows to the economy of Gateshead, many were made redundant, less money was spent in the town and more had to be spent on unemployment relief. Railway workers moved to Darlington, causing a sharp drop in population. Greenesfield shops did re-open during the war but closed once again in 1959.

The only large engineering firm to survive the trade depressions of the 1880s and 1930s was Clarke, Chapman. This firm was started on the South Shore in the early 1860s by William Clarke, an engineer who had worked for Armstrong at Elswick. New premises were taken on St James' Road in 1874. In the same year, Captain William Chapman, a new partner, joined the firm, followed three years later by C. A. Parsons. The manufacture of winches was the mainstay of the firm at first but Parsons experimented with turbines developing electricity and the firm also helped develop the carbon filament light bulb with J. W. Swan. Parsons left the firm in 1889. This now world famous firm concentrated on the production of marine auxiliary equipment until recent years when work on power stations led into nuclear engineering. Following a recent merger with John Thompson Ltd., the group is now one of the largest in the United Kingdom.

Chemical Works

Like many of Gateshead's industries, chemical

manufacture began as an isolated historical inci-
dent and the chemical trade is a typical example.
At the beginning of the eighteenth century a rather
mysterious person known as the 'Jew of Oakwellgate' is reputed to have manufactured compound
of cyanogen (a highly poisonous gas). Unfortunately, no trace of his activities can be found
today.

The chemical works in Gateshead in the nineteenth century were situated to the east of the
town, well away from the centre of population—
even in those far off days, the environment was a
subject of concern to those who lived near chemical
works. The first factory was started in 1827 by
Anthony Clapham who manufactured soaps and
soda. His works are best remembered for the very
large chimney which at 263 feet was the largest
on Tyneside. Such was the fame of this 'stupendous
work of art' that a song was written in commemora-
tion. The firm was taken over in 1858 by the
Jarrow Alkali works and again in 1891 by United
Alkali.

The best known chemical works are remembered
as 'Allhusens', developed in the 1830s by Charles
Attwood and bought in 1840 by Christian All-
husen who successfully expanded his business
until he occupied 137 acres of the South Shore.
'Allhusens' was incorporated as the Newcastle
Chemical Works Company in 1872 and this in
turn was taken over by United Alkali in 1891 and

production concentrated on caustic soda. In 1889, 1,200 men were employed here but from this date there was a gradual run down, which accelerated after the First World War, as the chemical trade was transferred to Teesside. By 1926 the premises were re-let as factories and even poultry houses and in the 1930s the great chimneys were demolished. One reminder of the past was the spoil heap estimated at 2 million tons which was still smouldering in 1951. Fortunately, a use was found for the lime as agricultural fertiliser, and the removal of $\frac{3}{4}$ million tons continued from 1953 until the 1960s. The remaining spoil has been incorporated into East Gateshead Riverside Park.

As could be expected, chemical works were unpleasant places in which to work; the heat was considerable and so the men were frequently thirsty. Boys were sent to local pubs for beer and rum while the landlord of the 'New Gateshead' was regularly disturbed by the night shift workers leaving work who hurled 'Irish confetti' (half-bricks) at the door to waken him. The work was dangerous, and burns were commonplace, although, surprisingly, fatal accidents were not numerous. However, the workers' health was frequently impaired by the heat and corrosive atmosphere. In 1891, the wages for this very unpleasant work varied according to trade, but the highest appears to have been £3 for a 42-hour week by bleach packers.

Glass and Ropemaking

As well as the more general engineering industries, Gateshead was the home of specialised trades such as glass and ropemaking. By the eighteenth century, there was a bottle works at the South Shore which later expanded to include the manufacture of plate glass, before it closed in 1840 after a life of about one hundred years. Pipewellgate was the centre of this trade, the first glassworks being established there in 1760 by Joseph Sowerby, at the west end of this street, followed in 1814 by Joseph Price and his Durham Glass Works (just west of Brett's oil works). Price later had an interest in another glass firm in the same street. Letters from Sowerby show the state of the industry in 1833: there were five glassworks employing about 500 men and £100,000 in capital. Skilled tradesmen worked an average of four days per week for £2 while labourers earned only 18/-. There was a decline in the glassmaking from this time but during the 1850s several smaller firms sprang up and some survived until the turn of the century when only two companies remained, Sowerby's and Davidson's. George Davidson established Teams Glass Works in 1868. Both manufactured moulded or pressed glass products, to give the impression of cut glass but at a lower price, and ornaments. Their local trade depended on hawkers who spent the night at the works and left in the morning, laden with glassware.

Sowerby moved to East Street in 1850 and in 1881 became a limited company, changing its name to Sowerby's Ellison Glass Works Ltd. In 1889 a subsidiary company, Gateshead Stained Glass Company, was formed, with the unusual feature that the principal employees were shareholders (an idea often suggested today as a means of curbing industrial strife). An example of the work of this firm can be seen in the 'King James' Hospital Window' in St Mary's Church. William Wailes, a celebrated stained-glass manufacturer lived in Gateshead; it was he who had Saltwell Towers constructed. The two firms of Sowerby and Davidson are still in business today, the former has carried on business for two hundred and fourteen years, the oldest in Gateshead.

Many industries on Tyneside needed rope— coal mining and shipbuilding for example—and a ropemaking industry started in Gateshead to cater for the demand. As early as 1691 a ropery was set up in Hillgate followed in 1795 by a more famous establishment at the Saltmeadows which in due course became known as David Haggie and Son. David Haggie had three sons—David and Peter, who became well-known in the public life of Gateshead, and Robert, who left to form his own firm at Willington Quay. In 1854 the Liverpool and Manchester Railway Company ordered a rope three miles long, eight inches in circumference and weighing thirteen tons. When com-

pleted, eighteen horses were unable to move the
rope which had to be taken up river to Redheugh
to the railway line. Wire rope had been made for
some years in a converted sawmill but a fire
destroyed these premises in 1873 and a new
building was constructed. Another fire in 1884
burnt down the hemp rope works and production
concentrated on wire ropes. The firm expanded and
in 1900 converted to electrical power. Production
rose, especially during the First World War, when
women were employed. They were known as
'Haggie's Angels' and were noted for their bad
language. In 1926 the firm joined the British
Ropes combine.

The other main rope manufacturer was Dixon,
Corbitt and R. S. Newall and Co. Ltd. These
were originally two separate firms with premises on
either side of the river Team, Newall's was on
the west bank. Both were established at the Teams
in 1840 and worked together for many years
before amalgamation in 1887. One of their famous
exploits concerned Cleopatra's Needle, Newall's
supplied the wire rope and Dixon, Corbitt the
steel caisson which were used to tow the obelisk
to London from Egypt by sea. Newall's were also
famous for the underwater cables which they
manufactured and later laid. Examples were the
Dover to Calais cable in 1850-51 and, more
important, from Suez to Karachi in 1859. The
amalgamated concern was taken over by the

Willington Haggie firm and in 1959 became part of the British Ropes Group.

Clay Tobacco Pipes

An unusual trade, the manufacture of clay tobacco pipes, was carried on in Gateshead. In fact, the town was a centre for clay pipe making, although this industry did not employ many men. Smoking was widespread in England by 1600 and although the first recorded mention of a pipemaker in Gateshead is 1646 in the burial register of St Mary's it is probable that this person, William Sewell, had been in business for some years. The peak of clay pipe production in the area was the nineteenth century when growth in population increased the demand for pipes; there were ten pipe-makers in Gateshead in 1838 but there were also many amateurs, such as publicans, who made pipes.

Shipbuilding

The Tyne has been a port and shipbuilding centre for many years. There have been shipbuilders at Gateshead in past centuries but none have been large enough to rival the giants of industry nearer the mouth of the river. Ship and boat building in Gateshead was centred on Hillgate and the river banks to the east of the town. Small ships and keels were the main vessels constructed and by the middle of the nineteenth century the larger

ships were being built in the Friars' Goose area
while boat building was concentrated on Hillgate.
Despite the presence of the large firms down-
stream, a slipway at Friars' Goose was in use until
the mid-1960s. Trawlers were launched here as
recently as 1961.

Shipbuilding has been a very minor industry in
the town, but there are two examples to show
that Gateshead men were to the forefront in the
development of steam power and iron boats. In
1814 a steam-boat was launched from the South
Shore and went into service on the Tyne. A
Gateshead glassmaker, Joseph Price, realised that
this new form of propulsion was here to stay,
bought shares in the ship in 1815 and was con-
vinced that steam tugboats would be profitable
to manufacture and sell. Unfortunately, his ideas
were not popular and he was almost bankrupt by
1838, but, still certain that this was the power of
the future, took out a patent for adopting steam
boilers for ships.

A letter in the local paper, *The Gateshead
Observer* in February 1860 stated that: 'The
first iron boat built so far as I know, was a rowboat;
in the year 1821, at Gateshead.' This was an
experiment carried out by an employee of Hawks'
with financial backing from Sir R. S. Hawks. The
boat, the *Vulcan*, was completed in 1822 and was
31 feet long. The following year it was defeated
in a race with a wooden boat and was being tested

and re-designed when the builder, James Smith fell overboard and was drowned. The cause of this was said to be the crew who had 'too much beer and too little ballast'. After this setback the iron boat was not developed and was allowed to rust away.

CHAPTER SEVEN

COMMUNICATIONS

Roads

Unlike the present day, roads were of very minor importance in Gateshead's historical past. As the town was very much smaller than it is today, there were only short stretches of road which also served as sewers and a place to leave other rubbish. As might be expected, they were often in a state of disrepair.

In 1555, each parish was required to appoint Surveyors of Highways as officers of the parish. These surveyors were empowered to call upon residents to work on the roads to prevent them becoming neglected but this 'statute labour' naturally proved unpopular and road works were only carried out when necessary: in 1633 the streets were 'made even at the King's coming'. A special rate could be levied to pay for repairs, but this was only done eleven times between 1633 and 1734.

From the end of the eighteenth century some improvements were made, due to the rebuilding of the Tyne Bridge. Church Street was constructed to alleviate the steepness of Bottle Bank, which itself was widened at this time. The Street Act of 1814 gave wide powers to commissioners to improve the streets in general. In Gateshead these commissioners included several well-known local public men, but despite this, they were not very active and paid more attention to lighting and watching of streets than to improving the road surface. In 1836 they transferred their powers, and debts, to the borough council.

When new streets were formed within Gateshead, they were taken over by the parish. From the mid-eighteenth century, main roads connecting large towns were known as turnpikes, under the control of turnpike trusts. Three such roads led into Gateshead; from Durham, Hexham and Sunderland, following the present routes of Old Durham Road, Derwentwater Road and Sunderland Road respectively. There were toll houses at Shipcote Lane, Windmill Hills and Kirton's Gate on the Felling boundary. The present Durham Road through Low Fell was opened as a turnpike in 1827, seventeen years after the idea was first put forward and the present A1 still follows this turnpike—apart from the new Gateshead Highway.

Turnpikes were in competition with the railways and lost revenue to this expanding industry. Many trustees lost interest and attendance at meetings was very poor, Nevertheless, the trusts struggled on in the face of mounting criticism about the state of the roads and pressure from the Home Secretary to wind up their business. By 1871 all the Gateshead trusts had relinquished their powers and all roads within the borough came under the control of the town council.

The present council has embarked on an ambitious road network to carry the ever growing volume of traffic through and around Gateshead. The Gateshead Highway has alleviated congestion in the town centre while the Western bypass from Eighton Lodge to Scotswood Bridge will provide a route around the town and a motorway link with the Team Valley Trading Estate. These modern road improvements are part of the redevelopment of Gateshead and have removed the criticism of the town being a 'dirty lane leading to Newcastle'.

Public Transport

The first public transport was provided by stage coaches, waggons and carts. Stage coaches operated between large towns but local services were carried out by the carrier's carts operating from public houses on High Street. The only major coaching inn was the 'Black Bull' which stood in High Street. The carriers served villages throughout Durham and survived until after the First World War when motor buses extended their services on these routes.

Public road transport in Gateshead began when the Gateshead and District Tramways Company began operations in 1883. Previous attempts to establish horse-drawn transport included an expensive hackney carriage service which began in 1827, with fares of one shilling per mile. Steam trams were used at the beginning of the service but in 1897 the British Electric Traction Company bought a controlling interest and electric trams were operating in May 1901. 'Stopping places' were introduced in 1904, and the first pay-as-you-enter system in Britain was tried in 1912. This last venture was not a success due to the added congestion caused at the Wellington Street terminus.

The trams ran to Heworth, Sheriff Hill, Dunston and Low Fell, while in 1910 new lines to Springwell Road and Saltwell Cemetery were opened. The system was very successful for some time. In 1908, 12 million passengers were carried and high dividends were paid but criticism increased, notably during the First World War. Boys were used as conductors, services were withdrawn without warning and the track was in very poor condition. The town council had an option to buy the Tramways Company and used this as a threat several times in an effort to improve the system. In 1916, a fatal accident at Bensham spurred the company to make improvements as did the threat of a government enquiry in 1920, but complaints were still to be heard. The corporation could not afford the asking price of £500,000 and the trams remained in private hands. Some modernisation was carried out and links were made with Newcastle over the High Level and Tyne bridges, superseding the horse-brakes which had run from 1878.

Trolley buses were introduced in Newcastle and the Gateshead Company planned the same innovation but the Second World War intervened and the low bridges on West Street and High Street prevented such a system linking Newcastle and Gateshead. Trolley buses were later abandoned in favour of motor omnibuses. An Act of Parliament in 1950 approved the conversion to buses and the days of the trams were numbered. The final journey was made from Dunston on 4 August 1951.

Motor buses had been operated by the Northern General Transport Company since 1913. The 'Northern' began as a subsidiary of the Tramways Company and by 1914 owned 54 buses. After the war, routes were expanded and soon covered most of North Durham. Several rival companies competed for passengers during the 1920s and 1930s until fare-cutting forced out the smaller firms and companies owned by British Electric Traction operated all the routes within Gateshead.

Criticism of bus services have continued, complaints being levelled at the lack of an adequate bus station in the town which meant buses travelled on through routes to Newcastle so Gateshead shopkeepers have suffered a fall in trade. Fares and cross-town routes have also been criticised.

In 1969 pay-as-you-enter buses were introduced on some routes and have proved more successful than in 1912. Concessionary fares were introduced in 1970 followed in 1973 by free travel for pensioners throughout most of the Tyneside area.

Railways

During the 1830s several proposals were put forward to build railways in north Durham. Companies discussed and vied with rivals for support for their own plans. Two companies emerged as the strongest, the Newcastle and Carlisle Railway Company and the Brandling Junction Railway Company. An agreement was reached whereby the latter would build lines from Gateshead to South Shields and Monkwearmouth and an inclined plane to join the former company's line from Blaydon at Redheugh. This inclined plane was constructed to give the Newcastle and Carlisle Company access to a coal staith at Hillgate; early railways were usually built with coal transport facilities in mind.

This short section was the first to be opened in Gateshead, on 15 January 1839. The line through the town followed the same route as the modern line across West Street and High Street. Apart from the main line, other visible parts of the Brandling Junction are the slope from Oakwellgate which led to Gateshead's first station, and the incline between the Redheugh and King Edward bridges. This latter was worked by a stationary engine but later by locomotives, as many as four being used to push and pull the waggons up the slope. This very noisy work went on day and night; it must surely have been a source of great annoyance to the residents of the area.

The railway was first planned to go under Gateshead. However, a bridge was preferred to a tunnel as the stations would not have been near the centre of population and the town would not have derived any commercial benefits had the latter plan been implemented. The arches formed by the bridge were let to small businesses to provide additional revenue, just as they are today.

The currently fashionable problems of 'The environment' are not new. 'Noise pollution' was discussed in relation to the bridge through the town, while the owners of Redheugh Estate were paid £6,000 for the land used for the track and station and an additional £2,000 as compensation as the estate had lost value due to the railway destroying the quiet seclusion of the area.

The Brandling Junction was bought by the Newcastle and Darlington Railway which later became known as the York and Newcastle Railway Company. It was this company that first obtained permission to build a line from Durham through the Team Valley, but this line was not completed until 1868, twenty years later, following virtually the same route as the present main line.

Railway facilities in the town continued to expand. Engine sheds and workshops were built at Greenesfield in 1852 and were extended three times, in 1854, 1867 and 1877. Gateshead West Station was opened in 1844 and Gateshead East in 1877. This latter station remains the only station in Gateshead, serving local passenger traffic only.

Gateshead did not enjoy good relations with the railway companies. The council made several requests concerning extra stations, workmens' fares and express services which met with little or no success. The York and Newcastle Company was taken to court in 1847 for failing to complete a new street near Half Moon Lane within the specified time but the council lost the case over a legal technicality. In 1932 the railway sheds were closed, bringing heavy unemployment to the town. All in all, Gateshead was badly served by the railway companies.

After the Second World War, the decline in rail traffic was countered in Gateshead by closing several stations. Low Fell closed in 1952, Bensham in 1954 and Gateshead West in 1965. The sheds at Park Lane were closed in 1959 and became a freight depot while in 1963 the Lamesley marshalling yards were opened. The railway industry in Gateshead is now a shadow of its former self but signs of its importance can still be seen; the locomotive sheds at Greenesfield, old Gateshead station now

used as railway offices, and the North Eastern
Railway engineer's house on Mulgrave Terrace,
now Greenesfield House health centre.

Canals
Canals were not built in the North-East for several
reasons. The industrial areas already had good
access to the sea, provided by the rivers Tyne and
Wear, while the spread of the waggonway system
would have made large capital investment in
canals uneconomic. However, plans were put
forward for a canal through the Team Valley from
Durham. A survey was made and the cost estimated
at over £77,500 with an annual revenue of
£25,000. Shares were issued in 1797 but work on
the canal was never started. Another proposal in
1803 to link Beamish Iron Works with the Tyne
via the Team Valley received very little support.

Bridges
The first bridge linking Gateshead and Newcastle
was built by the Romans in about A.D. 120 on the
site of the present Swing Bridge. It was destroyed
by fire in 1248 after eleven centuries of use which
included repairs and partial re-building. A new
stone bridge was completed in 1250, the cost being
borne by the city of Newcastle and the bishopric of
Durham. Each owned part of the bridge, the
bishop of Durham owning the southern third.
The boundary was marked by two stones, 'St

Cuthbert's stones', and later by one blue stone. There was a stone tower and wooden drawbridge at the Gateshead end and shops and houses on both sides. The drawbridge was replaced in 1770.

On 16 November 1771, a great flood destroyed all but one bridge over the river Tyne. The only one to survive was Corbridge. A temporary wooden structure was built and a ferry established while another bridge was built on the same site, but it was not until 30 April 1781, that the new bridge with nine arches was opened. In 1810 it was widened to allow adequate room for wheeled traffic but it was very low: keels were the largest boats which could pass upstream, and plans for a high level bridge were revived.

The idea of a high level bridge had been proposed in 1771, but this was disregarded. Several sites were mentioned, Redheugh, Rabbit Banks and Greenesfield, using suspension or conventional bridges. The main supporters of a high level bridge were the railway companies who saw such a bridge as opening a new direct route to the North. Obviously, the existing railways could not descend to cross a low level bridge. Robert Stephenson was consulted about the site of such a bridge in 1842 and a company was formed in which railway personalities such as George Hudson, the 'Railway King' were prominent.

The scheme received the royal assent on 31 July 1845, and work began. The first train crossed in

1848 and the ironwork was completed on 28 April 1849—Hawks, Crawshay were the contractors. It was tested by a special train in August and Queen Victoria formally opened the bridge on 28 September. The lower roadway was not completed until 5 February 1850.

As well as forming an obstruction to river traffic, the Tyne Bridge was becoming unsafe due to dredging by the Tyne Improvement Commission and in 1866 it was decided to demolish it. Another temporary structure was built while this was done and the Swing Bridge was constructed. This was the largest swing bridge in the world at the time and took eight years to complete. It was designed and built by Armstrong, Whitworth & Co. and came into use in June 1876. There were no tolls on this bridge, and for many years it was more popular than the High Level Bridge. People obviously did not mind a long walk down to the bridge and up into Newcastle if they could save $\frac{1}{2}$d toll.

In the 1860s, the idea of a high level bridge from Redheugh was revived and in 1865 a company was formed to promote such a bridge. The Redheugh Estate was about to be developed as building land and such a bridge would guarantee a regular income from workers crossing from the western suburbs to work in Newcastle. However, the North Eastern Railway could not be persuaded to help finance a second road/rail bridge and so a road-only plan was accepted, with the result that the project was not a great financial success. The engineer was Thomas Bouch who worked on the Tay Rail Bridge which collapsed with great loss of life. The Redheugh Bridge was opened on 1 June 1871, but required frequent repair. It was largely rebuilt between 1897 and 1901.

The next bridge was known as the New High Level until it was opened on 10 July 1906, when it became known as the King Edward Bridge. It was opened by King Edward VII. The North Eastern Railway was entirely responsible for this bridge which was built to give a straight run through the Central Station for North-South trains.

As early as 1893, a joint committee of Gateshead and Newcastle Councils was set up to report on the question of a new bridge from Gateshead High Street to Pilgrim Street, but a report advising against such a bridge on the grounds of cost was accepted by Gateshead council in 1900. A similar proposal was again vetoed by the council in 1904. By 1922 traffic congestion on the High Level and Swing Bridges was increasing. Tram lines had been laid over the former and there were fears that the increase in traffic would be too much for it and 'would be found some morning in the river'. River traffic was heavier than at present and the Swing Bridge was often open. Moreover, a bridge owned by the councils of Gateshead and Newcastle would not have any tolls.

In 1924 council meetings were in favour of a new bridge, public meetings were held and work began. Many slums as well as a few fine old houses were cleared in Gateshead to accommodate the bridge and its approaches. King George V performed the opening ceremony on 10 October 1928. Apparently an old man in the crowd had been present at the opening of the High Level and every other subsequent bridge over the Tyne. He was Moses Easton, aged 80.

The next important development concerning the Tyne bridges was the ending of tolls on the High Level Bridge (owned by the London and North Eastern Railway) and the Redheugh Bridge (owned by the Redheugh Bridge Company). They became toll-free on Coronation Day, 10 May 1937. There were well-founded fears that Gateshead would lose more trade to Newcastle and that the former town would lose a large contribution to its rates, paid by the London North Eastern Railway who were reported to be asking £250,000 as compensation for the removal of the High Level toll (in 1924 the railway company collected £22,000 from the tramway companies for their use of the bridge). However, a government grant helped towards the cost of acquiring the toll rights.

Today, in 1974, there are plans for a new Redheugh bridge, to be built to the east of the present bridge, and as part of the proposed rapid transit system, other bridges are to be built down-stream of the present Tyne Bridge.

The river Team has also presented an obstacle to communications. High Team Bridge was built in the 1880s, replacing a medieval stone bridge. Low Team Bridge, another early bridge, was reconstructed in 1905, linking Gateshead and Dunston. A second bridge built nearer the Tyne had been opened in 1875 but by 1925 it was considered inadequate but its replacement was delayed until 1933. It was officially opened on 17 December 1934.

CHAPTER EIGHT

PUBLIC SERVICES

Water Supply

The street names of medieval Gateshead, Pipe-wellgate and Oakwellgate show how the town was first supplied with water, although the exact locations of these early wells are not known. Wells and springs proved adequate until the seventeenth century when the formerly abundant supplies were interrupted by the sinking of many coal mines around Gateshead, and the authorities began to take an interest in water supply. The parish employed two pant masters from 1632 whose duty it was to maintain the existing wells in a clean and serviceable state.

To make up the deficiency in the supply, water was brought from springs on Gateshead Fell and Heworth 'in lead pipe downe to a pant (well) to be built for the use of the Towne'. At this time, Newcastle also needed more water and this was supplied from Gateshead. The land on the south of the Tyne is higher than on the north, an important factor in the gravity distribution system, which was the only method then available. In 1699

William Yarnold obtained an act of Parliament
to supply Newcastle with water from Heworth
Fell. Water from here was carried partly in an
open trench and partly in wooden pipes to two
ponds near the junction of High Street and
Sunderland Road. From here, the supply was taken
round the east of Holy Trinity to Oakwellgate,
over the Tyne Bridge in lead pipes and up into
Newcastle. A part of this pipe was found by
council workmen at Sunderland Road in May
1973. It was of wood, probably elm, three feet
long, weighed approximately three stones, and the
internal diameter was five inches. Although more
than 260 years old, it was still in good condition,
and some water was still flowing through it. The
pipe is now in the Shipley Art Gallery. In 1721,
only 22 houses had a direct supply of water, and
although the number increased throughout the
century, the majority of people had to carry all
their water from the wells. As the population grew,
and more water was needed, reservoirs were built
at Carr Hill and the end of Mulgrave Terrace in
1819 and 1844 while additional supplies were
taken from the Tyne in 1835. In 1845, the Whittle
Dene Water Company was formed and in 1854
it was superseded by the Newcastle and Gateshead
Water Company, the same company which supplies
Gateshead today. In 1845 only eight streets in
Gateshead were supplied with water. This
quickly increased to 51 by 1849 and about 13,000

of the population (out of 24,000) had access to a supply of fresh water in that year.

In 1833 a ten million gallon reservoir was built at Carr Hill and the following year, the supply from Whittle Dene was piped over the Redheugh Bridge. Water mains were laid through most of Gateshead and Low Fell, but the higher areas at Sheriff Hill and Wrekenton still had to rely on wells and springs for some years to come.

Police

Like the other early public services, the policing of Gateshead was the responsibility of the parish. Four constables were appointed each Easter, but as they were unpaid, it is reasonable to assume that they did not provide an efficient service. These constables were backed by the stocks, whipping post and the Tollbooth in High Street which served as a prison during the eighteenth century. A County Court was held on Saturdays in the Goat Inn, Bottle Bank. It was said that in this pub, a man (or woman) could get drunk, commit a crime, be arrested, tried and sentenced, all without leaving the building.

The number of crimes increased towards the end of the eighteenth century and in an effort to combat this trend, societies for the prosecution of felons sprang up. Three were formed in Gateshead, in 1774, 1789 and 1794. These societies paid rewards and prosecuted criminals in court. The members were property owners, shopkeepers, and generally those who had something of value which would attract the attention of the criminal classes. From the 1830s, the police force and courts improved and the societies declined in importance but after amalgamating in 1862, they survived in Gateshead until 1873.

The Street Act of 1814 had improved the policing of the town, watchmen were appointed to patrol at night from October to March and apprehend 'all suspicious persons'. In 1827 there were five watchmen and a Captain who received 10/6 per week each. The Tollbooth was superseded by a lock-up in Church Walk and then Bridge Street, though both buildings were in poor condition. Apparently a prisoner escaped from the latter in December 1843 by knocking down a wall! A new prison was opened in West Street, opposite the Town Hall, in 1848 and survived as offices until 1972.

Crime increased but so did the size of the police force which was appointed after Gateshead acquired a town council, in 1835. Six constables were appointed in 1836. They worked only on Saturdays and Sundays, but the watchmen were still employed to supplement 'the force'.

The main crimes dealt with were drunkenness and assault, although a report by the Superintendent of Police in 1850 painted a black picture of the disreputable boarding houses where 'the young vagrant comes into contact with the old and experienced thief, and where are discussed the plans and ramifications of the day'. Crimes increased throughout the century and it was common to lay the blame on immigrants, Scottish and especially the Irish. There was some truth in this allegation, but one must remember that they lived in the lodging houses which the police report criticised so much.

The size of the force increased to 18 in 1848, but there was a high turnover of men and a shortage of constables. They worked a 77 hour, 7 day week for 17/-, so it is hardly surprising that they left the force in great numbers.

The first two detectives were appointed in 1861 and by 1862 there were 33 constables at work in Gateshead. As the suburbs grew, police stations were opened in Askew Road and at Sheriff Hill, while the main station was generally housed in the same building as the Town Hall, on the site of Gateshead West Station, Mirk Lane, and finally Swinburne Street. During the first decades of the twentieth century, the main crime was drunkenness, with violent drunkenness common in the Teams area. The police tended not to interfere with battling pitmen and labourers wielding the buckle end of belts. After the peak year of 1924, when there were 766 charges of drunkenness, this problem decreased fairly rapidly and was replaced by offences involving motor vehicles.

In 1968, Gateshead Police Force, 214 strong, was amalgamated with Durham County Police on 1st October, despite protests which were not entirely sentimental.

Gas

Gas supplies to Gateshead began in 1821 from a gasworks in Pipewellgate, built in 1819. At first, the gas was used only for lighting streets and houses, gas fires, refrigerators and cookers were luxuries of the future. In 1838, Gateshead Gas Company was taken over by the Newcastle upon Tyne and Gateshead Union Gas Light Company, who paid £5,000 for the Pipewellgate gas works, and so began a series of disputes about the prices charged north and south of the river. Gateshead paid ten pence per lamp per week (there were 250 compared with 6,752 today), but Newcastle only paid eight pence. When the mains were extended, Gateshead Council had to pay for the new lamp posts and fittings whereas these were supplied free of charge in Newcastle. This favourable treatment of Newcastle was probably due to the fact that Newcastle Corporation had the power to establish its own gasworks. Although this never came about, the threat was frequently used to keep the company in line.

In 1876 the gasworks at Redheugh were opened on a 25-acre site at a cost of £100,000 and with additions, are still partially in use. The street lamps were lit by gas until 1948 when the gradual change-over to electricity began. One usually thinks of natural gas as a modern development. However, as early as 1840 there was a plan to supply Gateshead and Newcastle with natural gas from Wallsend Colliery, using the gas burnt off at the pit-head. The 'Spontaneous Gas Company' was formed but was short-lived and conventional means of supply were followed. Gas supplies were nationalised in 1948.

Electricity

The provision of electrical power and lighting for Gateshead was discussed by Council in 1896 but negotiations with the Durham Electrical Power Distribution Company were delayed for four years and the scheme was approved by the Board of Trade in 1899. The company undertook to lay power lines along the main roads within two years but were challenged by the Tyneside Electric Power Company. Eventually, the Council voted to support the Durham Company as the sole supplier for Gateshead and a power station was built at South Shore Road. This company supplied Gateshead until it was taken over by the Newcastle upon Tyne Electric Supply Company in June 1932. Electricity Services were nationalised in 1947.

CHAPTER NINE

THE VILLAGES

Low Fell

Gateshead Fell was a wild, largely uninhabited area, which for many hundreds of years formed part of the common land of Gateshead, under the control of the lord of the manor, the borough-holders and the freemen. There were pits and quarries scattered over the 631 acres which constituted Gateshead Fell in 1822, the year the Fell was enclosed. The people who lived there, tinkers, gypsies, pitmen and quarrymen, mostly occupied turf huts and on enclosure ninety of these were demolished, usually against the wishes of the owners.

The old Fell is quite unlike the town we are used to today. In February 1745, John Wesley, the famous Methodist leader, was travelling north to Tyneside when he lost his way in a snowstorm on the Fell. He later commented: 'Many a rough journey have I had before, but one like this I never had.' In 1770 Robert Hazlitt robbed a coach and postman near Beacon Lough. He was caught, tried and hanged at Durham and his body hung in chains on a gibbet at the scene of the crime to deter other would-be highwaymen. Sixteen years later, a Francis Russell 'one of the Gateshead-Fell gang' was whipped in Newcastle for his crimes.

However, after enclosure in 1822, civilisation came to the Fell. Drains and wells were laid out and the area became a select residential suburb, a striking contrast to a century before when in 1713 the cottages of the Fell paid an average rent of 9p per year, each! Large mansions, such as Heathfield, were built along Durham Road. The owner of Heathfield, a wealthy chemical manufacturer, was said to have kept bears in his garden.

The social centre of this growing village was the New Cannon where concerts, dinners and meetings of all kinds were held. The owner, Robert Clements, had been the proprietor of the Old Cannon on Sheriff's Highway but realised that the opening of the new turnpike would ruin his trade and so he built his new inn on the corner of Durham Road and what was then Buck Lane, now Beaconsfield Road. The 1880s were a decade of expansion with many more houses spreading out from Low Fell to Sheriff Hill, the Team Valley and Gateshead itself. Gateshead was expanding southwards in the Shipcote area but the rural views lasted until the Second World War. By this time, the residents were proud to live in Low Fell as opposed to Bensham or Teams and frequently omitted 'Gateshead' from their addresses even though they lived outside of the ancient boundaries of the Fell. Surprisingly, this attitude is still found today, but Low Fell has changed into a bustling suburb with many shops and very heavy traffic, a contrast to the peaceful days when children could play marbles on Durham Road in perfect safety.

Wrekenton

Wrekenton, or Wreckington, was named by the Rev John Hodgson after the Roman road called the Wrekendyke which passed to the south of the village. As part of Gateshead Fell, the area was desolate and in 1822 Wrekenton consisted of a row of cottages, built in 1815-16, a large house and a public house. The area was inhabited by tinkers, pitmen and quarrymen. After the Fell was enclosed and divided in 1822, real growth began. A hiring of farmhands and other servants was held in March 1822, and subsequently every April and November. It was the only such gathering for several miles and was usually accompanied by sideshows, sports, roundabouts, clog-dancing and, of course, drinking.

Wrekenton grew rapidly during the years 1825-35 but the provision of public services did not keep pace with other developments. The roads were very poor, lawlessness was rife and standards of public health deteriorated badly. After several explosions at local mines the pitmen refused to return to work with Davy lamps and were laid off. Many left and were replaced by tinkers and tramps, 'until the village became headquarters for all vagrants in the district, men, women and children, with donkeys, pigs and dogs, all crowded in the same room, demoralisation, filth and crime, abounded'. As a result of this, the slums of Wrekenton were attacked by epidemics of typhus and cholera. These tramps and vagrants were blamed because of their insanitary habits and houses and about thirty families were driven out by the villagers.

Wrekenton remained virtually unchanged for many years. In fact, the slums and old houses were not demolished until 1938-40 when much of the old village disappeared; Wrekenton Row and the courts and lanes behind the Ship Inn. Today the village character is no more as hundreds of council owned dwellings surround the Old Durham Road.

Carr Hill

Surprisingly, Carr Hill was once a small village isolated from Gateshead and Felling. There were several industries here, windmills, brick, pottery and glass works accompanied by the inevitable public houses and, from 1856, a Methodist Chapel. By the turn of the century, the working-class houses had expanded to Carr Hill and a large council estate was built from 1921 so that the only re-

maining traces are a stone terrace on Carr Hill
Road and the cottages at the end of Elgin Road.
The width of Carr Hill Road as it passes the site
of the village suggests that there was once a
village green.

POPULATION FIGURES

1548	1,670	1784	7,350
1576	1,800	1791	6,840
1621	3,135	1801	8,597
1631	3,381	1811	8,782
1641	4,038	1821	11,767
1651	4,470	1831	15,177
1661	4,449	1841	19,843
1671	5,019	1851	25,570
1681	5,967	1861	33,589
1691	6,135	1871	48,627
ca. 1695	7,000	1881	65,845
1701	6,036	1891	85,692
1711	5,715	1901	109,888
1721	5,841	1911	116,917
1731	5,817	1921	125,142
1741	5,343	1931	122,447
1751	5,490	1951	115,017
1761	5,400	1961	103,178
1771	5,550	1971	94,457
1781	5,940		

Figures for years before 1808 are estimated

LIST OF MAYORS

1835 George Hawks
1836 Michael Hall
1837 James Pollock
1838 John Barrass
1839 William Henry Brockett
1840 William Hymers
1841 George Sowerby
1842 Robert Davis
1843 William Kenmir
1844 Thomas Cummins
1845 Thomas Cummins
(second term)
1846 Thomas Revely
1847 John Cuthbert Potts
1848 George Hawks (second term)
1849 George Hawks (third term)
1850 Joseph Robson
1851 Charles John Pearson
1852 John Lister
1853 David Haggie, jnr.
1854 Richard Wellington Hodgson
1855 James Smith
1856 George Crawshay
1857 Bryan John Prockter
1858 William Brown
1859 George Crawshay (second term)
1860 James Hewitt
1861 Benjamin Bigger
1862 Benjamin Bigger (second term)

1863 George Crawshay (third term)
1864 Isaac Charles Johnson
1865 Edmond Crawshay
1866 George Miller
1867 Robert Stirling Newall
1868 Robert Stirling Newall (second term)
1869 William Brown (second term)
1870 John Marriner Redmayne
1871 Richard Wellington Hodgson (second term)
1872 William Muschamp
1873 George Charlton
1874 George Charlton (second term)
1875 William Galloway
1876 William Galloway (second term)
1877 John Walton Robinson
1878 John Walton Robinson (second term)
1879 Edward Smith Hind-marsh
1880 Edward Smith Hind-marsh (second term)
1881 William Affleck
1882 William Affleck (second term)
1883 Robert Rankin
1884 Thomas McDermott

1885	Thomas McDermott (second term)	1912	John Maccoy
1886	George Davidson	1913	John Maccoy (second term)
1887	George Davidson (second term)	1914	William Edward Wardill
1888	John Lucas	1915	William Edward Wardill (second term)
1889	John Lucas (second term)	1916	John Maccoy (third term)
1890	Silas Kent	1917	John Maccoy (fourth term)
1891	Walter de Lancey Willson	1918	John Maccoy (fifth term)
1892	Walter de Lancey Willson (second term)	1919	William Clough (second term
1893	William Henry Dunn	1920	William Clough (third term)
1894	William Henry Dunn (second term)	1921	Sir John Maccoy (sixth term)
1895	John Tulip Scott	1922	Sir John Maccoy (seventh term)
1896	John Tulip Scott (second term)	1923	Sir John Maccoy (eighth term)
1897	William Clough	1924	Thomas Peacock
1898	Francis Joseph Finn	1925	Thomas Peacock (second term)
1899	John Bradshaw	1926	William Edward Wardill (third term)
1900	Alexander Gillies	1927	William Edward Wardill (fourth term)
1901	Alexander Gillies (second term)	1928	William Edward Wardill (fifth term)
1902	Walter de Lancey Willson (third term)	1929	William Hall
1903	Lancelot Tulip Penman	1930	William Hall (second term)
1904	Lancelot Tulip Penman (second term)	1932	Jonathan Hodgson Ritson
1905	Lancelot Tulip Penman (third term)	1931	Jonathan Hodgson Ritson (second term)
1906	Alexander Gillies (third term)	1933	Timothy Armstrong
1907	Alexander Gillies (fourth term)	1934	Timothy Armstrong (second term)
1908	Alexander Gillies (fifth term)	1935	James White
1909	Alexander Gillies (sixth term)		
1910	William John Costello		
1911	William John Costello (second term)		

1936	James White (second term)	1955	Frank Pattison
		1956	Allan Henderson
1937	William John Pickering	1957	Abraham Crossley
1938	William John Pickering (second term)	1958	Joseph William Roberts
		1959	William John Pike
1939	Peter Strong Hancock	1960	Elizabeth Ann Hardy
1940	Peter Strong Hancock (second term)	1961	Christopher Hetherington Wheatley
1941	John George Orton	1962	Mary Bell
1942	Mary Gunn	1963	Thomas Wilkinson
1943	Sidney Alfred Heppell	1964	William Collins
1944	Thomas Ryan	1965	Robert Ninian Baptist
1945	Henry Kegie	1966	John Coulson Snowdon Wheatley
1946	Norman McCretton		
1947	William Finnie Barron	1967	Albert Victor Turnbull
1949	Charles Richard Flynn	1968	Charles Ryans
1950	Stanley George Bell Tyrrell	1969	William McKelvie Colligan
1951	James Arthur Hutchison	1970	Joseph William Roberts (second term
1952	John Thomas Etherington		
		1971	William Collins
1953	Michael Grant	1972	Frank Conway
1954	Ben Nicholson Young	1973	Leslie Carr

INDEX